THE MOM EGG

10

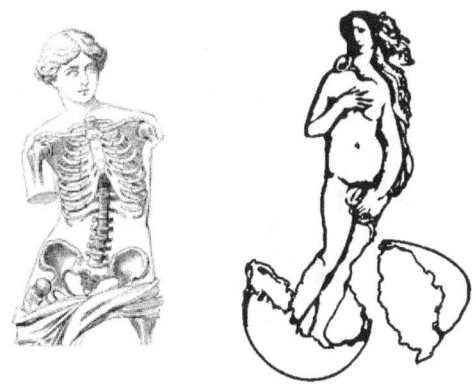

THE BODY

I speak two languages, Body and English.

--Mae West

THE MOM EGG

2012 Vol. 10

THE BODY

Edited by

Marjorie Tesser

Half-Shell Press
New York

The Mom Egg

Half-Shell Press
New York

The Mom Egg, an annual collection of poetry, fiction, creative prose, and art, publishes work by mothers about everything, and by everyone about mothers and motherhood, and is engaged in promoting and celebrating the creative force of mother artists, and in expanding opportunities for mothers, women, and artists.

The Mom Egg is a member of the Council of Literary Magazines and Presses.

This publication has been made possible, in part, by a grants program of the New York State Council on the Arts, a state arts agency, and the Council of Literary Magazines and Presses. The Mom Egg is extremely grateful for this generous support. The Mom Egg is also grateful for the assistance of The Motherhood Foundation. With gratitude to founding editor Alana Ruben Free and founding publishers, Joy Rose & Mamapalooza. The Mom Egg logo was designed by Suzanne Altman.

Cover image "Moon Dancer #17" by Edward Walsh. www.walsh-sculpture.com.

ISBN-13: 978-0615596440 (Half-Shell Press)
ISBN-10: 0615596444

The Mom Egg
PO Box 9037
Bardonia, NY 10954

Editor - Marjorie Tesser

Website: www.themomegg.com
Contact: themomegg@gmail.com

CONTENTS

i

Photographs:

Helen Ruggieri

FOOT POEM

dusk settles into the glass
                     that looks out
                     that wants in

I watch my feet
                     my handsome feet
                     my pink toes
                     strip of white
                     over the arch
                     where the strap crossed

oh pretty feet
                     oh pretty pink toes
                     oh dusk in the country
                     beating on the glass
                     small winged insects
                     writing in thocks
                     on the screen

       you have such beautiful feet

Sandra Florence

DRESS OF BLUE LEAVES

My boundaries are fixed like pins in the border of a half-made dress, a dress of blue leaves and summer afternoons. My mother is at the sewing machine stitching the dress, closing the apertures of cloth and color against space, sealing the sleeves, running the white thread across the borders of the dress. The dress is whole and finished. Now she is ironing the dress. A starched and ironed dress that falls across my legs creating a shade in the heat of the afternoon, the long silence of heat that fills the valley, moisture diffusing sunlight and a door opening somewhere down the street. There's a smell of clean cloth and warmth rising from the ironing board. Hemline, trim, border, edge. My mother goes over the edges, the borders, again and again to make sure she hasn't missed anything. She is careful to press the edges down, to know where one thing stops and another begins. Sometimes she lifts the iron across the dress and it touches both sides at once, the part of the world that is only the dress with its dotted-swiss trim, and blue leaves, the long sash that will wrap around me once I am in it, and the part of the world that is not the dress, where the border dissolves away, where there is only remembrance and longing.

Kathy Engel

Blue chiffon you

cascade down my salted
cocoa muscled
back in deep isosceles
colliding where the
round begins
you skirt my jutting
kites, blue chiffon
you slip my hilly hips,
I trot you into sandy orange
dusk, walk your scallop shore
skim your foamy tide
I taste your musk, my breasts
discuss their milky past
you graze my belly wider blue
you mingle with
my hair that was a movement
in itself, its auburn jazz
now tame, oh blue
chiffon I swim the big
Atlantic in your wave, my
brawny shins, my long
articulating toes,
my scarred and serious ankle
bone, its wars, my hinge, you grace
the sadder tunnels with your sweep,
this waltz, blue chiffon.

Kathy Engel

WHAT I'M MADE OF

I am a crab I am
chemical dispersant
spill, I am spilled
spilling, fish swelter
stone, I am slick, eyes
burn bleed oil, nose
oiled mucous, talk
spits from my oil
swollen lips, gurgle
and sputter drip from
my ears, crude ruts
my cheeks, neck scar
leaks oil, hair sheens
nipples weep yellow
collostrum oil, my
gut gasses, hips sling
through oil, thighs, wrists
calves oiled, ovaries
discharge oil, ankles
shellac shells, feet
smudge oil, I cough
up oil, skate oil loose
oil bowels, dna splits oil
blood scabs oil
bay of oil fin of oil rooster
crowing oil crow cawing oil
oh crab, oh oil of bird

Gulf Coast Oil Spill, Summer, 2010

Barbara Crooker

MANET AND THE SEA

title of an exhibit at the Philadelphia Art Museum

The Escape of Rochfort, 1880-1881
Who cares about those convicts rowing a path in the moonlight?
It's the water we want to look at, taking its own sweet time
as it steps up to the microphone to solo, an improvisation in blue:

Ohio match tips, mouthwash, flax fields in France.
The moon, once in a while.
The moon, where I saw you standing alone.
The moon, forme d'Ambert, Roquefort, Stilton, Gorgonzola.
Speedwell, rosemary, chicory, plum.
Skies, smiling at me. The wild yonder.
Something about a Monday. Something to get tangled up in.
Twelve bars, Bessie, Billie, Janis, piano, steel guitars.

Oh, Eddie Manet, he's got the blues,
got paint on his shoes, done paid his dues,
oh, Eddie Manet, he's got the blues,
yeah, he got them blues so bad . . . . .

Toni L. Wilkes

COMPOSING

Her fingers wander over,
a volume of gilt-edged sharps
swirl through the house—
flats splutter out & vibrate.
She explores foot pedals
with her hands. Not long ago,
she played flat-palmed.
Now she fingertips keys,
cracks the lid, slides the top,
to expose the strings that
fire to her hammers—
taps currents that rise in waves,
vast oceans swell to her
rhythmic renderings absorbed
by the swish & thunk of wires.
Hammers damp when her
foot toes the pedal. A wind
howls through her palms
& starfish-like, her hands
smear spirals, design ciphers.
Like a whale whose call
chisels waves, she throws
herself onto fluid melodies
where they crest & spill.

Carol Levin

THE CHAMBERS IN SYMPHONY HALL

The crush in the lobby is alive with life and death
debates: Brahms vs Bruckner, tempo and temper.
Before the lights blink you illustrate the essence of life,

gesturing how our heart is connected to the ups
and downs of our diaphragm;
how each breath moves our heart.

This body of work scored
for two keyboards is relentless
with certainty, thrusts rhythm

into the air. My body serves
two masters when the imperious
chords of a sixteenth note

octave surge and oxygen
vital as melody heaves through my
respiratory tract conducting air

filled with grace notes
into my bronchial tree
snagging breath in hidden surfaces

on the little pockets of my lung.
Nowhere in the body
does the outside world

with all its creatures of microscopic
dimension have such easy access
to the sacred interior cavities.

Inhaling the climax of the main theme
the nubile rhythm undulates
my diaphragm, dances my heart

suspended in its pericardial sac.
My senses stand erect inhaling
the essence of life as earth grinds on its axis.

.

Golda Solomon

MAP DOT
after Nikky Finny

Not privy to me,
It went twenty plus eight years unknown to me
Although I knew all too well wherein it laid
IT remained my mystery

All intact, I'm sure.

From the tender crudity of names called,
I could infer that it was good.
Wrinkled, almost invisible
But to the touch, wrinkles engorged
Flirted, engaged, demanded satisfaction
Bad girls spread knowing lips
This aperture capable of moistness
Was to me distant as Antarctica
My map dot wanting to be touched.

Jacqui Morton

BODY AFTER CHILDBIRTH

I ovulate on day thirteen
and I know this

because

on that day
I can have an orgasm
while sitting in traffic
if I move the right way.

Eve Packer

CECIL ON THE DEUCE

(1)

ebony is 5' 11"
beautiful body
blonde wig
right abdomen:
old cig burn,
right deltoid:
cut-scar

shes working her way
thru pharmacy school
at l.i.u. stripping
down behind the glass
door, doing what you
ask for---10 bucks
& up---

at showworld

    water/
    sky/
    fall
    down/
    part of
    earth/
    to
    grind
    up/
    crush
    heart
    mesh
    flesh

      a
    true
    bird journey

(2)

lisa has stretch
marks, and when she
turns her ass, massages
her labia, you can see
shes had an episiotomy,
can move the muscles
of her vagina lavender lipgloss
nails---slip 2 bucks
thru the slot---

the window comes down at playbox video

    murdered bird
    girl
    thats my
    rain name/
    all hands
      to me/
    so when do
    i go

    true
    sun
    water
    moon i love you
    i like you
    gonna go
    see you
    bye

Susan J. Allspaw

TWO MEN WRESTLING
for CF

In the botanical gardens   with boys
dressed   as men
who laugh   at the sculpture
of two men   wrestling
because they think   men
should laugh at such
suggestive   poses
when they are men
wrestling   in what seems like
love
because love   in men
is awkward   for men
dressed   as   boys

But if it   were women
wrestling in that sculpture
the men
        would look
                and look
and silence would fall   like a blanket
hiding   their jealousy
        or awe
at such love, or
        at such wrestling
                between
                        two women
because what they want
        is more
                than just stone
more
        than what they see
in the shade
        of eucalyptus and pine.

Nina Schuyler

MOTHER

"Run along now," said mother. "Quiet time."

To her son Daniel, these words meant being bored to death for what felt like years and years, as if he were being punished, but why should she punish him? He was a very good boy, that's what she said this morning after he choked down his horrible hard-boiled egg and oatmeal and bitter black tea.

"Daniel."

He slowly pushed back his chair and plodded down the long hallway. This was in 1951. Years later he would look back at this day as the one that changed how his mother saw him, as if he wasn't what he appeared to be, as if it best to put some distance between them, the day she discarded her dreams for him and prayed he'd be okay.

He plopped on his bedroom floor. As he built a house out of Lego, then leafed through his dinosaur book, he could feel her in the house, though he heard nothing, only the steady click of his clock. Slowly he opened his door. As he crept down the hallway to the living room, the air became vivid and heated and everything seemed more alive when he saw her stretched out on the red plush couch, a white cloth over her eyes. Her long fingers were woven together on top of her stomach, her tall shoes that tapped on the wood floor side-by-side on the carpet. He loved her so much his whole body shook with a well of emotion. More than anything he wanted to lay on top of her, fill himself up with her fragrance, and rub the soft white underside of her arm.

Maybe he whimpered or let out a sigh because she took off the cloth. Her face was no longer smooth and warm, but narrow and pointy like a hammer. "Daniel. Go to your room. Mother needs her rest and so do you."

But he didn't. He was a big boy now and didn't need a rest. He trudged back to his room and stood at the window. The neighbor's little black dog with bright white teeth was yapping at a bird, as if telling it something.

He found himself in his parent's bedroom. The big bed with the cream-colored bedspread and fluffy pillows. He'd never been in here alone. Father's closet with stiff suits and leather belts and shiny black shoes and the smell of shoe polish. And mother's—her fragrance of flowers and lemon rushed out, enveloping him, pulling him inside. Her wispy white scarf with pink flowers, soft like the underside of her arm. He wrapped it around his neck, tucking his nose into a fold so he could breathe her in. Her soft pink sweater with milky white buttons, buttons smooth and cool against his tongue. He took off his shirt and put on the sweater. It stroked his bare chest and back and a spasm ran through him so hard it shook his whole body.

When he reached for her green silky skirt, it moved like her, like water. He undid his trousers and tucked the top of the skirt in the elastic of his underwear so it hung in ripples to the floor.

He knew he shouldn't be here, knew he should be in his room, be a good boy and play or rest or watch the little black dog with bright white teeth, but he couldn't stop himself. Reaching into her coat pocket, he found her lipstick and rubbed it over his lips. Like she's kissing me, he thought. He closed his eyes to remember better her smell, her touch, her fingers stroking his cheek, and he felt she was everywhere for him, in the air, in the light, seeping right into his skin, and he lay down on the floor in a tight ball, knees tucked to his chest so she could hold all of him, which is where she found him when quiet time was over.

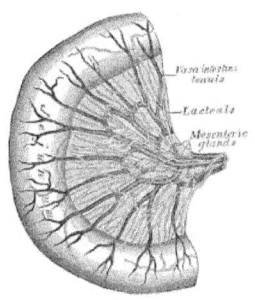

Virginia Bell

THE WORKSHOP

*We might chart the itinerary of womb-envy in the production of a theory of consciousness: the idea of the womb as a place of production is avoided both in Marx and in Freud. ...
Everywhere there is a non-confrontation of the idea of the womb as a workshop, except to produce a surrogate penis. --Gayatri Chakravorty Spivak*

Some nights he tucks a small pillow,
a soft globe of the earth,
under his night clothes

and curls around his belly to hug
the world,
to be hugged out

from the inside. He used to experiment by day

with his pregnancies:
balled up laundry, a plastic bowl.

Just as we swim until water is warm,
until the cries and shouts
from the pool's edge

are muted by circles of amnion,
muscle, fat, pulled skin,
until moving horizontally is normal.

In bed on a cold afternoon, we pull up
a sheet and blanket

(and some of us stick our feet
out the bottom for air
because some of us came into the world that way).

We insert some piece of ourselves
into some orifice of an other: a nose into an armpit,

a tongue into a navel, a finger
into an anus, a penis
into the dip of a belly

or the back of a knee, a mouth onto another
mouth. Some nights

he tucks the soft ball under his clothes
and I marvel

that all he makes all day is not enough:
additions, divisions, sound
now pattern, words now lyrics,

running now rounding the bases,
how long it takes to freeze a glass of water,

the gathering of inflection, gesture,
and mood that make
a person.

If it were enough, would we tunnel into the earth
under channels of water,
kneel in halls to put our heads back down,

would we gather in dark rooms to drink?

Ellaraine Lockie

ON BECOMING GEORGE SAND

A stick from a crabapple branch
in my seven-year-old surgeon's hand
The boy prone on a bed of grass
Pants pulled down and burnt toast eyes
big as the pubescent fruits on the tree

I wanted one of what my patient had
when what I had down there was empty
My mother caught us and paddled me
with the stick

Later I'd learn the term penis envy
Feel the weight of that appendage
in my dreams, study Freud
Someday I'd wear baggy pants
Stuff a fedora with a head of brown curls
Ticket-pocket with a pack of Camels

Sneak out into the night
sans the shine of cosmetics
come-on of skin
cat-in-heat call of perfume
Instead, the courting of fragile hands
that hold pen or paintbrush
The smoky side of rooms
with a piano bar
The counterpoint of a nocturne

Lani Scozzari

BROTHER

One night quiet as Neptune, I climbed into your crib
and your eyes did not ramble, blurry-dimmed from hunger but centered on
mine—

A moment hard as a nucleus, secret and unkillable.

How I longed—

To hoard your neon cry, kiss your droughted body an ocean—

Before her door bent the jam, before her quick jagged shuffle clipped the tile,
before her mother-fury, fierce as a sea blizzard offered you a pulse.

The brink of my skin not yet grown and your lips, bursting
rose hips. My body burned.

Motherness plucked rapid across my tight veins.

I gathered your flailing
limbs, nuzzled your gumming mouth against my chest, concave— could my body
feed you?

Nancy Vona

THE LICE CLUB

My friends and I are at the local cougar watering hole on Thursday night. I listen while they--all mothers of girls--vent about head lice. I am the mother of boys and deal with nose-picking, penis warfare, and gleeful farting contests, but no head lice. Over glasses of chardonnay and pinot noir, my friends describe what it's like to be a member of the lice club: the call from the school nurse, the agonizing process of picking each nit out of the hair, the family line-up to search for lice amongst the hair of dad and siblings. Only the dog is exempt from the line-up. In some cases, the moms hire professional nitpickers to purge lice from themselves and from their girls. My friends emphasize the need for better lice awareness in the community and compare education campaigns for lice removal in public versus private schools. A line has been drawn in the scalp and the lice are winning.

My head begins to itch. I sip my pale ale beer and scratch my hair when my friends are not looking. These women--successful book publishers, entrepreneurs, account executives--are humbled by these parasites. The lice don't realize that they have targeted the families of talented professional feminists. They just want a warm human body to feed on, a place to rest their lousy heads. For us, the lice remind us that we are both human and animal, whether we like it or not.

Jack Kristiansen

NAKED

maybe drink, maybe money	w
(excess or shortage)	e
can make a body shameless	l
maybe grief, maybe art	c
maybe hormones, maybe war	o
(winning or losing)	m
maybe aging, maybe joy	i
but for certain birth	n
the bloody work of birth	g

Katie Manning

REALITY

My breasts
ache, swell
as if
each one
were growing
its own
baby inside
My body
(mind, some
thing)
is misplaced
I sleep
sleep
There is
nothing else

Molly Sutton Kiefer

RISING

You feel like driftwood, caught in a current.
Your fingers trace lines along the low swing of belly,
you remind me you are more than bubbles boiling up
from a pot. I caress you because it is instinct; I do it in public
so they can know my belly is more than a barrel,
I've grown so because I am two.
It's the quiet times I notice you most:
reading in a hammock, summer filaments,
hours after plucking berries from a branch.
You want to tell me something: *it's dark in here,*
or *please bring more water to me,* but all I can hear now
is that swish of current, the tide inside the tide, the belly rising.

Molly Sutton Kiefer

BEACON

Naked, I mistake the criss-cross of nursing bra stripes
for new stretch marks. I count them in circles,
and when I bare my belly to my startled husband,
which I do a lot, knowing he must will his eyes to not pull away,
he'll whisper, *That looks like it hurts,*
meaning those angry purple marks,
the ones that look a result of violence,
a lynx striking me twice, once on the left,
then the right, reaching toward
the place he misses the most. This is the only piece of me
that does not hurt like hell:
my knuckles are swollen and bruised,
my hands tingle without a woolen brace,
my knees scoff at perpetual motion, my uterus kicks back.
My body isn't meant to be like this,
or perhaps my brain circuitry doesn't connect
the buried goddess of pregnancy to my own misshapen waddle.
I've bent chairs to matchsticks,
sent sheaves of paper tumbling at every turn.
And every day, I grace the bathroom, my hips swinging,
restless legs seeping into every joint, my shoulder, my toes, and bend
and spit and repeat, remembering what I thought was safe before.
Naked, I walk across the beaded floor,
I relish the way that hump leads the rest of me,
a beacon, a little node, a flash of light beneath my skin.

Felice Aull

DAUGHTER IN HER EIGHTH MONTH

Approaching the predicted
midpoint of her life
she is now profoundly pregnant.
It is her first, and no technology
was needed, only the hormones
released by love and a watchful womb.
Grandmotherhood approaches,
a state I did not crave, just as
I did not crave to be a mother
until she thumped her way
into my world, as now her fetal girl--
that floating fingered shadow
the ultrasound detects,
detecting lack which means
she'll have a daughter too--
is pummeling her.
That's how our babes enlist us.
I feel the tiny fingers pull me
into, through, blood on blood,
we three are sliding, slipping toward
the edge of separation.

Rosalie Calabrese

PREGNANT

Those last three months
of pickles dripping brine
and aromatic spices
fresh from the barrel,
potatoes fried to a golden turn
in the fish market's bubbling oil,
ice cream covered with walnuts
and frozen chocolate sauce,
I watched your father put on weight.
Now, as your wife feeds her cravings,
and it's you who's growing baby fat,
I'm swelling up with joy.

Anelie Crighton

PREGNANT WITH MEANING

Pregnancy, as experienced, is not a metaphor, but a challenge: those solid thumps to the ribcage are reminders that much as you might like to think of yourself as a brain on a stick, an intellect tethered to the complex technology that is the body, you are in fact a placental mammal. You need to work? No, you need to nap. You want to stride along like you always did, long straight steps, fast and confident? By week 30 it will be all you can do not to waddle.

My walking mantra is, 'There is nothing wrong with your legs. There is nothing wrong with your legs.' This is strictly true. There is, however, something wrong with my feet (swollen), pelvis (slowly disconnecting), lower back (hurting), stomach muscles (stretched), blood pressure (low) and brain (sorry?). My horizons have gradually contracted. My slow pace and ready fatigue make the ten minute tram ride into the centre of town seem the equal of a day-long trek. At home I must intersperse activity with rest, reaching for another glass of iced water while I prop up my comically puffy feet. I feel hot all the time, and am immensely fond of very cold drinks and ice cream. Very cold ice cream drinks are also acceptable.

The tenant has been excellent company. Once his movements were detectable at 22 weeks, his wriggles and stretches and somersaults were delightful. While he still had the room he moved rapidly and erratically, brief flutterings and jabs like the strangest indigestion you've ever had. As he's grown, his reachings have slowed, become more definite, more obviously in response to changes in his environment. Any time I lean forward, a small foot firmly reminds me that he does not appreciate cramped lodgings. I have pointed out that at 5'10" I offer quite spacious accommodation, but the kicks continue.

One day my husband caught a glimpse of me dressing and said in wonder, 'You look beautiful.' I found this astonishing; I look like a woman who's swallowed a basketball, perhaps to distract attention from her thick ankles and dry hair. I have had a protruding belly for months yet still misjudge my movements, my round new boundary regularly encountering table edges and door frames. Numerous sleepless nights have hung a crescent under each eye. The fit of my voluminous maternity pants gets a little more snug each week. There is beauty here?

Observed and observing, one's progress is constantly at issue - are you gaining weight, feeling worse, sleeping less? Is the baby growing longer and fattening up, does it move ten times an hour twice a day? Once you've exhausted the present, the future beckons: that unpredictable day (early? late?) when the contractions begin, and the x hours thereafter when you'll breathe and relax and finally make up your mind about an epidural. The days to follow with the fragile and confused newborn, the nights of crying and feedings. And just wait 'til they're a year old! Or 18 months! Or two years! The early months will feel like years, they say, when they're not saying it will all go by so fast. Parenting is asynchrony.

What a rude shock this is, this memento corporis, this foregrounding of flesh-and-blood. Our social selves are fundamentally intellectual, personas sprung from the mind which connect through the invisible media of speech and sight. We are our words, our views, our status updates - until pregnancy, when the body reasserts itself. It has a formidable arsenal to bring you down: faintness, fatigue, pain, squeezed lungs: all of these are more than equal to your conviction that you can carry on as though your ballooning midriff is a minor inconvenience. Sure, march up that staircase - just don't expect to get to the top without puffing like a steam train and feeling dizzy. Keep working or studying, but be ready to embrace synonyms and dead-ends, distraction and sudden blanks. A new patience with yourself is required, a temporary accommodation. Because the fact is, you're extremely busy. Under the surface you're assembling genes and cells, connecting neurons and testing muscles. Science-fiction factories of precision parts could only dream of replicating with your efficiency. Pregnancy has evolved from being an accessible miracle, a blessed mystery bestowed upon us by a benevolent creator, to seeming the supreme technological achievement, an inbuilt instruction set of vast complexity which draws millions of parts into just the relation required to produce a new thinking, feeling person. The terminology might have changed, but our awe is the same.

And so the due date looms, and I am working my way through the last chores and warily witnessing what new discomforts my body devises. The pivot-point of birth separates the weeks before, which are trapped beneath a net of plans and appointments and checklists and advice; and the weeks after, nothing but a huge blank, a cute stranger with incoherent needs, a new life for him, for my husband, and for me. A challenge, indeed, which will forever re-balance the relationship between mind and body.

Matthew Miller

PARTUS

Riflebutt the curve of her wool
socked foot into the shoulder shove

her knee down now toward her ear fingers
wrapping hamstrings stretched

now like pulled stitches
that birthmark on her knee
the flaws called the fall now

on the other side of the bed the nurse locks
hairy arms around the other leg

just a spit of chemicals
a pathology of the lonely
love now

know this if it's needed as old men
not her real doctors crouch into her
crotch now a naked spider
in the limp of fluorescents

residual feelings would be natural
aches of addiction
but hungers fade get replaced

walk out right now
into a dead stomach winter
at this hour of the morning no one cares
for what disappears forever

the baby now by heaving rips out
brown and beet now
so much more rip and twist
from thighs lights her hot swell of earth

focus on the scissors the slick purple
and grey of the cord
now so much black

blood should there be so much
black blood and no crying

starched hush then little hacks
at air the chokes on spots of oxygen
how long now since the water

broke how many times do you need
to say now in a hospital
not now stop now please now

not breathing right he says *emergency now*
what is it she says

leave now before anything
can be lost in the scraping

at air *yes it's a girl*
is she all right now which she

the doctor digs rubber gloves back into her

more bleeding down here than I like
to see scissors thread now
old hands snip now winces rip

her face now *see if she's okay make her*
be okay she says now

run down a hall as if hip deep in mud
walls implode NICU doors blow

open into a pool of blue swimmers
too small for March now don't feel
bad feeling good she is not one

of them *now this way daddy*
someone says and now her eyes
open staring wet and we are

breathing right here terrified beautiful
now for what the world will take

Ariana Nadia Nash

EACH TIME THE NIGHTMARE COMES DIFFERENTLY

Sometimes I'm babysitting
and the baby's head falls back
snaps open like a hinge and I know
she's died in my arms Other times
I'm a mother and I peer over the crib
and see her ruddy face turned purple-blue
One night I drop her Another night
she chokes and I stare helplessly
And what I want to know is this—

is my therapist right—is dropping a baby
like dropping a ball—some dream sign
that I haven't taken responsibility?
Is this my body whispering I'm barren?
Can it be the random firing
of synapses? Will the dreams stop
reiterating? And can I ever forget
how delicate a neck is

Christine Redman-Waldeyer

NEST

in the cradle, emptiness -
not because
there was never a baby,
not because
the baby never needed sleep.

All the while
my arms stronger
for the lifting,
the letting go,
the reaching,
holding
rocking.

Rachel Dorroh

WE ARE WAITING FOR MILK

The baby boy yellows while the
breasts cast a non-committal gray.
His eyes shift under thin skin. His
mother's lips twist again, and then
mother and child stay quiet and still.

Let us hold her! Let the memory of
making milk beat in our hearts and
flow through the hands we place on
her back and under her hand holding
his head. Let the tempo of the milk
and the mouth be remembered
in our skin, and let her mind
let go its reigns.

Jessica Dyer

SO PIRATE, SO MOTHER

I have gone into it. I feel so *pirate* in all
the sparkle and flit and I've forgotten how

to fly, how to lick the clear juice from honeysuckles.
I have lost my fairy wings and hair bells,

my bracelet of shrunken skulls, my feathers,
my fool's gold. I am curling all my toes

and got my eyes stuck crossed. My eyelashes
fall out too fast for wishing these days. I will name

all my sons after saints, will hear the swooshing
of daughters caught undersea, under crinoline

and tapioca, will feel so mother inside, with all
the bread pans, the little poofs of flour shooting up.

Leah Mooney

ALL AFTERNOON

All afternoon, light has barely grazed
that sky, down-ward choked with snow.
You lay atop of me, heavy
with sour breath, fevered head
crushing into my lips.

Sometimes, what my heart is,
is a fruit split open.

What flows from it
flows into you. I think
how quiet it is,
this medicine. How it
soaks beyond
what is fibrous,
and bone-- and--

when I close my eyes I see nothing
but plump ferns. Fronds unfurl in song;
you drift into that tender sleep. Can you hear them?
I breathe. Hear them sing! Hear them,
that most verdant,
quiet song.

Leah Mooney

FIRST FROST

2: 00 a.m., when she has to pee,
my daughter whimpers, unzips
her pajamas, steps barefoot
onto floor. Suddenly,
the whole world
is cold.

We have woken with tongues
slowed. Words are
just another exertion
against our own bones.

While I wait, I hear
the tree sap slow. Blood, too
slows; by tomorrow
the skin of tomatoes
will have split

open and crows
will make off with red gelled
seeds in their beaks.

I bite down each
second before she
hops, flushes,

burrows her arms
in to the flannel and we

cross, the two of us,
into that season
where everything clings

to the last, burrowed,

tea colored hours.

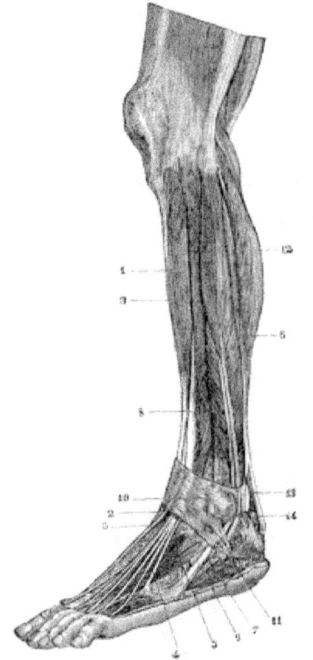

Kate Falvey

HUNTING AND PECKING AT THE NATURAL HISTORY MUSEUM

Skin is merely
skin
and a baby,
fierce with colossal
exuberant unrestraint,
can leave aggressive,
unmalicious marks with
teeth that penetrate
the true succulence of
joy. Ambition
to move
is inborn. The air
is torn
as if it were
a skin.
Language
is movement
and the air splashes
with the unbound
leap and frolic of
forming linked significances,
dimensional, alive,
furred and growled,
snake-like and avian.
The tongue takes for granted
its own
greedy participation
in the awful rouse of
genesis and
extinction.
And there is nothing of plight
about it. Jibbering
and jiggling, scratching,
and mowing, stretching
cadences out like limbs
swiping at a vine, the sheer

vented doing of it,
the vaulted pre-cambrian bones
humming their cathedral importance
in eons overhead.
Howls down a hallway --
ripe fruit splitting on glass --
rebound in red
and purple solids,
pulpy, extravagant,
the skins and nectar of
release.

And then the cases come
because they must
and poses are struck,
preserving a stiffened homage
to the feral, a hide
gnawed to a gamey suede,
a jackal bayed
with pointed stones and shrieks,
a circle of new flame singeing
his snarling, frustrate insistence.

The baby's hands slap
the separation
between fright and fur,
framing a clean story with
his tuneful eyes. He
notices breasts and
expressions. He
wants the dowager with her
flinty hair to have
what she is reaching for. He
wants to know
why she is crying, though it
may be that
she is simply
old and the tears
are a trick of our own
removal from her age. I
see them,
for instance, only

because the baby
has pointed them out.
To me she looks
sorry and unromantic, like
the ground has been hard
for a long time, like
she has never had enough
to chew on
or to keep her
unexposed, like,
in the conventional eyes
of her maker,
she is mythically
pitiful, the once
and future
hag.

My arms are
another kind of fruit
and the baby
tucks into them,
his giggles salivating
lustily, having taken in
giants
while holding
my hand. He has
deduced scale
and, amidst mastodons and
stegosaurs, and tortoises
big as wishing wells dwarfed
by fallen meteors and paled
by the fantastic lunar interiors of
ordinary minerals, he
is his own blast,
the force and fiber
of this succulent world.

Miriam Axel-Lute

WALKING AWAY UP THE WALL

They say geckos can walk straight up walls
using quantum physics.
They don't so much stick as bond,
their touch so fine it coaxes electrons from their orbit
and then sends them, overwhelmed, swinging away again
a plus and minus dance where atomic eyes stay locked
until the gecko's toes curl up and the angle of its attention shifts.

When you were five months old
I suddenly became obsessed with
the softness of your hands.
It was weeks until I realized
this was because you had begun to touch me—
the fist on the end of your windmill nursing arm
had melted to a stroking palm
resting like a kiss on my breast.
Your grabs for thumb or nose were
flavored with intention, not just reflex.
Like a stone wall under a gecko's pad
I bent toward the impossible
expanse of your fingertips every time,
organs lurching out of place
lead foot pumping out the oxytocin
trying to pin you to me with subatomic force.

You are nine months old now
and today I realized your dalliances
with floorboards and stacked plastic crates,
alphabet blocks and the pages of
The Very Hungry Caterpiller
have brought your body out of Eden:
Your palms have roughened.
  What an absurd thing to say!
  There is no trace of roughness in them.
And yet, they are rougher.
They have become matte with identity,
boundaries forming across the fractal tenderness,
edges the eyes can focus on and say

that is where I end and you begin.

Ana Garza G'z

ON THE UNVEILING OF THE STATUE OF ST. ANNE

The man who made her says, "She's beautiful."
His voice catches as if he's never seen
her, as if the hours of wax and metal casting never happened,
as if the flagstones beside the church laid themselves, blooming
the concrete circle at their center and the woman with the girl
both spontaneously emerged, standing
in a puddle of flowers, looking out
for her husband's car in the parking lot.

She's tall and slender, her shoulders squared
under a cloak, carded, spun, woven, and fulled
by herself with practiced fingers over weeks
at hours set aside for that, behind the girl
she also made, as carefully, as slowly,
as practically, in moments also set aside.

"You've got to see her," he says, stopping
abruptly, Conscious he's talking to a blind woman.
He resumes, "Touch
her face, her hair." He runs out of words
then, repeats, "her face,"
as if the outline of meaning can be read only there.

So I climb
into the planter, step
through the flowerbed, spreading
my fingers over nose, mouth, cheekbones,
eyes. When he is satisfied, I drop

my hand to the girl with the narrow shoulders.
They're squared too, and fragile
from hungry winters and bones young enough to bend,
but her back is as straight
and her chin is as certain,

and at her shoulders, the mother's hands,
too big and square to be
her own. I wonder

if the hands are actually their maker's, caught
somewhere in the act of shaping--wrists cocked,
knuckles in curved rows, fingers wide
apart like the branches of a shade tree, nails blunt
from hours of giving form.

"Yes, that's her daughter," he says
from the stones below, not noticing
my fingers on the woman's thumbs.
"Her face," he prompts, when I linger.

But my visual memory is far
too dull to trace the roundnesses and lines
 of innocence in the girl, the angles
of accounts kept
faithfully, life fulfilled,
marriage in sorrow, whatever else in the woman.

For me, it's the hands, the mother's
Or the maker's, open
Above the child, poised to push
the girl forward or catch her stumbling back.

Kelli Stevens Kane

(10)

when I was five
I used to rise up out of myself and watch me from behind.
I told my mama,
and she stayed calm.
I told my mama,
and she let me double.

Danielle Jones-Pruett

SUSPENDED

I hope one day my son skips school, hides flat
in his tree-house, backpack for a pillow

as the bus pulls away. He'll be giddy
in the morning, king of the treetops,

surrounded by comics, gum wrappers, small
sticks for fire. By midday he'll be bored.

Wondering what his friends are doing
he'll remember he has no lunch. He'll start

to notice details: a face in the tree
bark, knots the right size for a knuckle-bone,

the way dust settles, like a spirit all
around him. Cold in fall shade, he'll stretch

his hand to sun—take in how fingers burn
red around the edges. He'll sleep a little,

but not completely. He'll still hear squirrels
scratching above him, the call of birds, footsteps

in the leaves,—as he lies there, caught between
waking and dreaming—the sound of his heart beating.

Maya Jewell Zeller

CONSIDERING A SISTER

The other evening I considered
a sister for you. I considered this as
the snow fell and filled up the dark spaces
between each blade of grass
until beneath streetlights the lawn
was a field of gray and bright spots,
then until we could no longer see
the grass at all. Inside me an egg shifted,
I could feel it gliding
the small places of my body,
wanting to be a moon
with a tail. On the floor you moved
your blocks and trains, your clothes and owls
into a large pile. You like to collect
things in one room, to stack them
one on top of the other. You say who, who,
to your owl, stroke its head, hold it close.
Then you put it with everybody else,
make a family. Your doll you lay down
last, cover her with a blanket,
your body bent over her,
your face pressed to hers,
sing hi baby, hi baby, softly, these words
you can say, these two words you know
both soothe and mean love.
You can't say she's sleeping, yet,
you don't say shh. The houses
of our neighborhood, too, slowly
turned white and quiet, gave in
to the great possibilities of night.

Christine Stewart-Nuñez

LIGHTING

On the MRI, I see how God has wrapped
my son's brain in light, how He holds
it in His hands—a glow around gray

folds that house fiber-optic threads
of blood, webs of capillaries. Lightning
storms along synaptic clefts during seizures;

brain cells spark, flare, fire, surge.
In the nightlight's shine, I've seen
sweat soak his hair, my son's body

rigid. Sometimes cheek muscles twitch,
an arm jerks. Or, like the afternoon I held
him in a highway's ditch— brown and stiff

autumn grasses poking out of snow—
his legs were limp, the dark wells
of his eyes locked heavenward as if

in supplication. I leaned my preschooler
on his side, caressed his perfect skin.
You'll be fine in a minute—my mantra

until I persuaded even the blue, blue cloudless
sky, its cold breeze folding into April's
awakening fields. The light of that MRI,

the light of those fields—I see them
in my son's eyes when he cracks a joke,
when his words spark like fireflies

at dusk. That light holds me steady
when his jaw clenches, when vomit
is forced through his nose, when we spend

three silent hours in the emergency room,
when he steps out of the hospital, looks up
at the quarter moon and yells "Yahoo!"

Hannah Craig

CHANGELING II

That's the fifth lard-soaked hack
of bread. Sixth strip of bacon. The kid
who's never satisfied demands
another cup of whole milk yogurt,
more berries, more grapes.
A cantaloupe, still soft from summer rain.
And then a box of Cheerios.

A growing boy, they say. Milk pours out
by the gallon. The bear is growing in his brain.
Something that sleeps, sleeps, wakes up to eat.
At night I start up to find, at the foot of the bed,
cake in each paw, the back-bent shape
of a growl. He's uttering how
there's not enough left, there's not enough.

I am starting to lose my mind. He's out
in the kitchen again, shuffling from drawer
to drawer, stacking up the cans of beans and corn.
Open, he begs. The world will not. He drowns it down
with limeade and tea. I'm sick of how it goes.
The puff of his tummy through stained night-clothes,
the white-bark of his oily skin, the terror of an unending feed.

What he wants, he needs. The doctors say to count
calories or carbs. I'm down on my knees counting beasts
I've seen come and go, the pigs feasting on acorns,
the blue jays emptying out the feeders on the lawn.
Nothing this desperate is mine. Nothing this hungry
could be.

Dallas Woodburn

SUSTENANCE

After the daughter leaves, the mother develops a problem with food. There is always too much, or not enough. There is never the right amount of food in the house after the daughter leaves.

Before there was a daughter, back when the mother was not a mother, just a young woman living on her own in a medium-sized city, working a series of temp jobs and searching for herself in other people but never finding what she was looking for, back then her refrigerator was always empty except for beer and batteries and a carton of eggs, and her pantry was filled with nothing but Pop-Tarts and cereal, and maybe a couple Hershey's bars, hardening, white around the edges. Back then, the mother went whole days consuming nothing but stale coffee and grilled cheese sandwiches from Stu's Diner down the street.

She bought a basil plant on a whim because it was a sunny day and the basil smelled good and she was feeling optimistic and full of beginnings. She carefully picked and washed the basil leaves and made watery pesto linguine for her boyfriend's birthday. When they broke up two weeks later, the basil plant was already wilting on her windowsill, and the daughter was already growing inside her, though the mother didn't know it yet.

Then, one drizzly spring morning, the mother awoke craving a huge salad with dark leafy greens and cucumbers and ripe tomatoes, the crunch of fresh peeled carrots and broccoli, and nothing was the same after that.

The mother got a job as a receptionist at an orthodontist's office. Stu's Diner became a grease-smudged memory. She bought The Joy of Cooking and learned how to dice an onion. She learned to squeeze fruit for ripeness and she searched food labels for organic and natural. When bananas went spotty, she baked banana bread; when apples went soft, she peeled them and cored them and ate them anyway.

The daughter arrived with her own opinions. She preferred pears to applesauce; sweet potatoes to carrots. She adored Cheerios until, one day, she didn't. On Saturdays, the mother took the daughter to the farmer's market and together they filled the back seat of the mother's Honda hatchback with bell peppers, zucchini, squash; blueberries, peaches, raspberry jam. The daughter grew.

The Tooth Fairy came. In summertime, the daughter picked the biggest watermelon and insisted on carrying it to the car all by herself. They stopped at every other parking meter so she could rest. "Why don't I carry it for a little bit?" the mother said, but the daughter shook her head and set her jaw and lifted the watermelon to her chest. "No. I can do it." So they stopped-and-started, started-and-stopped, all the way to the car.

Twelve summers later, the daughter moves across the country. She lives in a college dormitory and carries a plastic tray around the dining hall for breakfast, lunch and dinner. She calls the mother every weekend. The mother always asks, can't help but ask, "Are you getting enough to eat?"

"Yes, Mom."

"Are you eating enough vegetables?"

"Yes."

"Make yourself a salad. They have a salad bar, right?"

"Yeah, but I gotta go, okay? I'll talk to you later."

The mother eats salads every day, but still there is too much food. In her fridge, the lettuce grows mulchy, the bell peppers wither, the tomatoes turn fuzzy with mold. It seems the world moves faster than it used to. It seems everything is decaying. She used to whittle away entire Sunday afternoons at Stu's Diner, slowly filling in the crossword puzzle with block letters. Now even her grocery lists are written in sloppy fast cursive. She eats lunch in front of the glowing computer screen and dinner in front of the glowing television screen and she chews quickly, automatically, not really tasting anything. When her plate is empty she feels astonished at how it all disappeared so quickly.

*

In two weeks, the mother is flying out to visit for Parents Weekend. When the daughter is taking a shower, the mother will open her mini-fridge and peer inside, hoping to find blueberries and yogurt and string cheese. But she knows she will likely find the fridge of her own youth. She can picture the Pop-Tarts under her daughter's bed, the sugary cereal, the potato chips. The mother will throw the daughter's sour milk in the trash. She will buy the daughter apples and hug her and tell her she loves her, and then she will board a flight back to the mid-sized city she once thought was a shithole but now loves as home, leaving the daughter to her own shopping and eating and not eating.

The mother will set her bags down in the hallway and open her familiar fridge. She will slice the tops off the strawberries and wash the dirt off the grapes and sit in the sunshine of her kitchen and chew and swallow and chew and swallow and savor every bite.

Lucia May

ELLERY AT NINETEEN UPON RECEIVING HER TWO YEAR MEDALLION

Your birth brain
seemed perfect
except that
you always
craved more
food and touch.
You writhed
and screamed.

Your urges became
your commands.
No one could
give enough.

You decided
to survive.

Your birth heart
has learned
to sate
your own soul
for today
with love.

Kathleen Flenniken

BROODING

for my oldest

I stretch out on the stainless steel tray
that is this sleepless dark
and examine my own maternal sensors
tuned half a world away to your blinking light.

Imagine arrays of radio scanners spinning
while the blip that is you
strolls cobbled streets in Spain.
I read you very clearly.

Thank you for shifting one pair of underwear
from your suitcase to your carry-on
before we checked your bags and said goodbye.

What do I do with these feeler things
once they outlast their usefulness?
Like extra hands getting in the way.

Before you were born
I let go of your stroller in a dream
and watched you tumble off a cliff.
They were just emerging then.

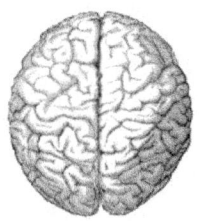

Judith Skillman

CAUSE AND EFFECT

If I wind up my hand
it will play a song. No, listen,
if I get down on my knees
and beg, if underneath the ferns
there are insects with voices,
some big-celled argument
comes true. Behind the grimace
in cold Spring the word romance,
if I wind up my hand.
A certain cruelty thrives.
Beneath the forest floor spongy
with mushroom-laced spoors.
After the canopy of the trees
beings with extra shadows
copy themselves onto trunks
and water. The comb holds
our sex, and the pattern of violence
makes and mocks us.
If I wind up my hand
it will play the tune
you wanted to hear.

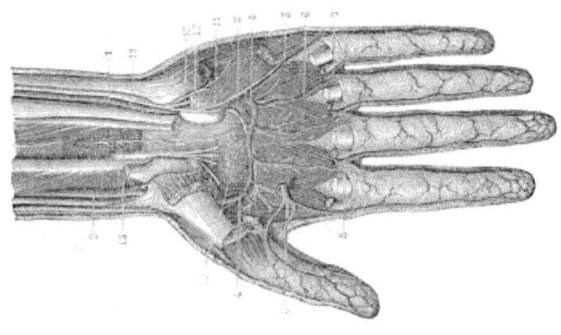

Valentina Cano

KALEIDOSCOPIC REJECTIONS

You pointed with a finger dry as chalk,
outlining a vague idea,
something that had grown feet,
and a mouth full of teeth.
Nothing I said made a difference,
not the words stitched carefully
with chamomile, yellow, delicate,
prone to nervelessness.
Not the smiles
pinned like insects to a board.

We stuck to each other,
not knowing which door to open,
where to point the ax
made of whispered offers
and compressed breaths.
With a shrug like wind ruffling a tent,
I moved away,
leaving you pointing,
wide-mouthed,
at the sky.

Sharon Charde

FEASTING ON OUR DETRITUS

Clara said you would feed on what
some people call love for years.

What will you eat first?
The Rilke poems I read you—
the chapel you said was ours?
My hand in your mittened ones—
the silver bracelet I brought from Italy—

my red car?

God must be broken into smaller pieces,
my body, that jar of history, smashed—
I would have joined you at the repast
but you've already swallowed my teeth.

In the dark dining room of loss
rests a plate, a napkin unfolds.
I light the candles, fill the glass—

leave hunger's map for last.

Teresa Tumminello Brader

(W)HOLE

Filling one of her orifices
with one part of his body
is no longer enough. He yearns to crawl inside her.

He wants to miniaturize his whole body, insert it
into a less obvious entry point—for instance, the fenestra of her ear—
then slide down the walls of her capillaries
and swim in the bayous of her blood.

If she learns how to shrink before he does,
he'll put her in his pocket,
stroke the whole of her
with the pad of his thumb
all day long.

Carl Palmer

CHURCH RITUAL

warm unmoving august air
morning mass uncomfortable
pew folded hands in lap no
fidgeting odors of too many
flowers over perfumed women
yellow smoky incense keeping
focus downward feeling mother
stare as she leans looks closely
with a sigh unclasps shiny red
leatherette handbag releasing
familiar aromas smelling salts
lipstick pink compact powder
rattle of keys coins cellophane
locates least wadded tissue
wets corner with nicotine spit
attempts to wash new freckles
from my sunburned cheek

Lesley Dame

REVOLVE

Even in adulthood, your heart spreads
its hot little fingers in every direction,
doing the natural thing. You think maybe
your body needs both dark and light.
Something about balance; it somehow
makes sense. In the winter there's always
room for more warmth. You just want
to be whole. Your heart just wants to be
the biggest, best heart on the playground,
climbing up and down monkey bars on a
sunny day; you like to influence other hearts,
make them feel good. Maybe you're a bitch.
Probably. But you just want love, you
want everyone to feel love. You want to be
the sun, and you want planets and moons;
you want windmills, and all things that revolve.

Jessy Randall

THE HORRIBLE SHOULDER PADS OF LOVE

When the
horrible
shoulder pads
of love
slip down
to your waist
and make you
even lumpier,
you witness
the flickering
of fluorescent
longing, buzzing
with frustration
and perhaps
joy

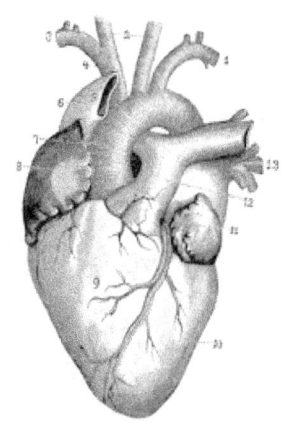

Melisa Cahnman-Taylor

POET TO THE REJECTING EDITOR: ON SENTIMENT

We have halted, heaved, counted breaths, closed eyes and pushed
wet, slinky words growling onto breasts for fattening. We've riddled
with silken hairs, rhymed with defecations, swabbed what hurt, shushed
what wasn't needed. Not to disturb the direction of dreams, we swaddled
them then gave titles before they could walk. We sent them laden
with lunchboxes and stamps before they, or we, were ready.
And we praised them: first pull up by bedrails or their whole weight
laid out on white sheets, safe enough to tip toe away.
We've pampered these poems, and like them, we've whimpered
for never-ending cartoons, soft served scoops, and one last good-night
kiss, then another. Like you, we've wanted to silence them, solicited
sleep. We should be grateful for your wish to unburden our plight:
hormone-heavy poems, a few too many pounds of sentiment.
Your rejection only thickens our tendency to stain and swell.
Even if, as you suggest, the poems seek starker climates,
even if suddenly or gradually they bid us farewell,
they, like you, will never stop calling us: mother.

Holly Day

YES I KNOW

my husband comments on how I've let myself go
since we've been married, how ever since I've had the
kids, I've gotten fleshy and old. I want to tell
him how I have to look this way now, that if I
was still young and beautiful

I could never leave the house. if I looked even
the slightest bit attractive when I left the house
I would attract other men and maybe I would
probably cheat on him.

and I don't want to hurt my husband and I don't
want to hurt my kids-- if I looked like I did when
I was 20, if I was even a little
bit beautiful, I'm dumb enough I might blow all
this.

really, this charade of frumpiness is a
sacrifice I made for domesticity, these
glasses are designed to hide the blue of my eyes
this nasty sweatshirt and matching sweatpants hide the
fleshy curves of my hips and ass and the still-nice
breasts meant only for him.

Kelly Bargabos

WHEN I LOOK IN THE MIRROR AT EIGHTY

When I look in the mirror at eighty, I will see an alabaster crown adorning my head - each strand representing a birth, a death, a victory, a loss, a year of life, the passage of time. In the tired gray eyes I will see a reflection of every orange and gold sunset I have witnessed; I will see the bright pink azaleas of my home state and the dark green trees that I've been able to watch grow from a seedling. I will hear my laugh in each chiseled line and consider the grief I have survived. When I look down at my brown-spotted hands with purple veins, I will feel the soft coat of an animal they nursed back to life. I will taste the sweet flesh of a tomato from the garden I planted and tended with those hands. I will recite the letters they've written and finger the countless buttons they've sewn. I will be amazed that although they look worn, they are as strong as they ever were. I will look down at my breasts and see my babies cradled there as they suckle life from me. I will see the faces of women who have lost them and be grateful they are still part of me. And although they are retreating further and further away from me, they still make me feel like a woman. I will look down at my round belly and see it bulging with the life I once carried inside me. I will remember the pleasantness of a full stomach, enjoying a hearty meal with people I love and be glad for temporal earthly pleasures. I will look down at my feet anchored by toes with stubborn, yellow nails and I will see every inch of road beneath me as I walked to school, among distant lands and native streets, danced down aisles, every mile of the journey. I will feel the gritty sand and cool water they have tasted. I will be amazed that although they ache under the weight of all they've carried, I can still place one in front of the other and move forward. When I look in the mirror at eighty, I will see those who've gone before me – my mother's smile; my sister's cheeks; my brother's nose. I will relish the honor it is to carry the likeness of us, our family, into this age. I will recognize the young girl looking back at me and not be surprised that her spirit still inhabits this body. It is she who sustained me – to rise at dawn when I didn't think I could face another day, to stay awake all night when it was necessary. When I look in the mirror at eighty, I will see me and realize that as long as there are sunsets and tomatoes, there is something to see.

Linda Lee Ortiz Hughes Bakke

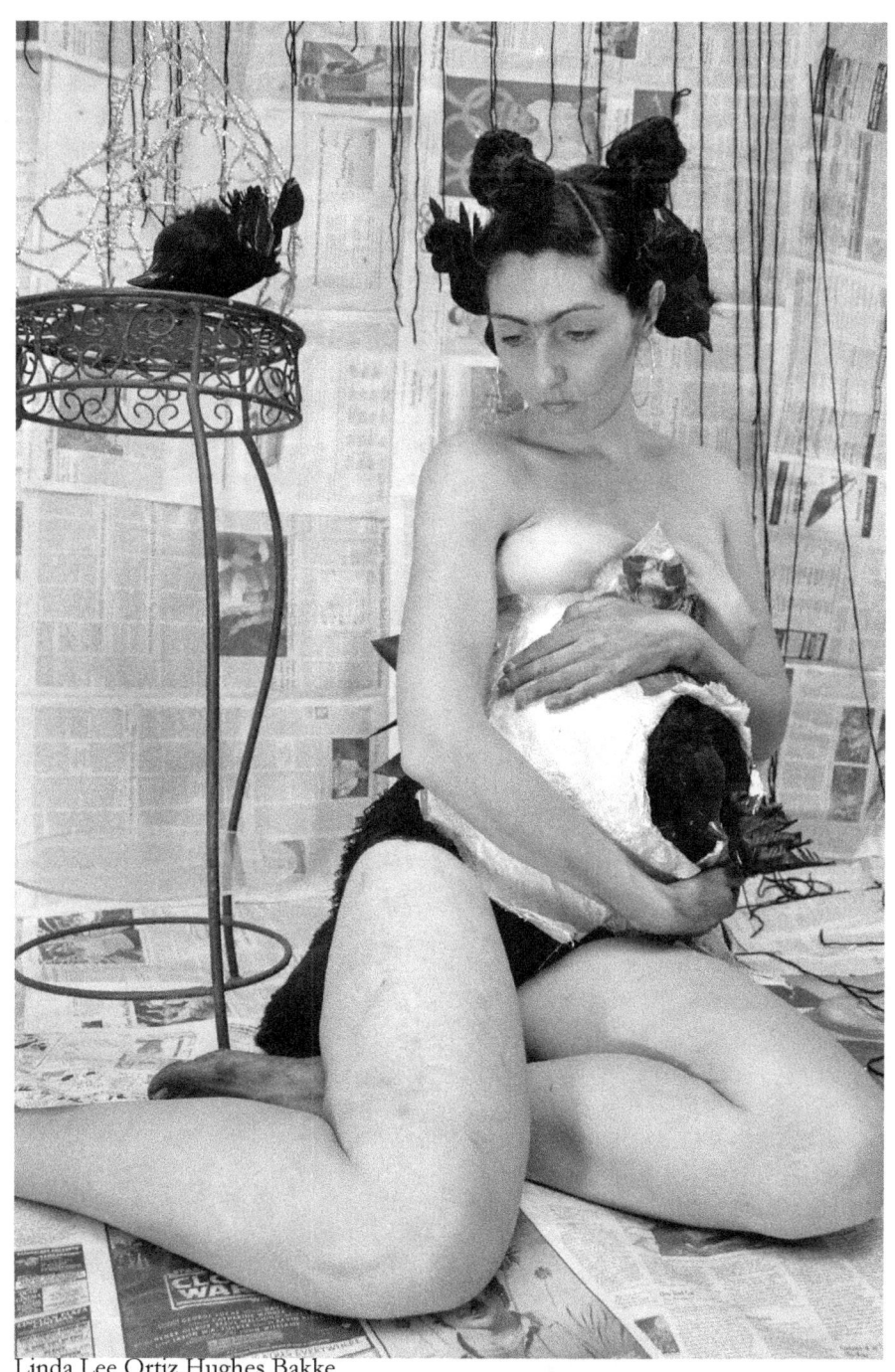

Linda Lee Ortiz Hughes Bakke

Nancy Gerber

HAIR

My mother and I are having lunch at a café.

My mother says, "Why don't you do something about your hair?"

I am 36 years old. I have two children.

"It's so wild and frizzy. I liked it better before."

My mother is impeccably dressed: wool slacks, sweater,

blazer, scarf, gold chain. I am wearing jeans and a denim shirt.

"Can we order now?" I say. "I'll have a tuna sandwich."

"What about a salad? I thought you were watching your weight."

"I'm in the mood for tuna."

"We never talk to each other like mother and daughter, like Ruth and Janet.

Why can't we be close?"

"We're close. We're close enough," I say.

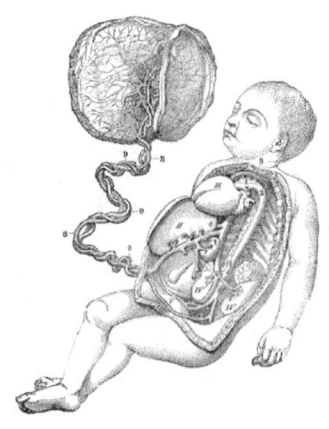

Kimberly Dark

MARILYN'S SMILE

I sympathized with Marilyn Monroe for her smile.

My mother gave me smiling lessons when I was a child.
I was older than I when I received hand-shaking tutelage,
younger than for tips on feminine smoking, that's for sure.

"You have a beautiful smile."
She began.
"Some people's mouths show too much gum above the teeth --
so you don't want to smile too big.
You can fix that though, if you're aware of it."
I was in my bed, nearing sleep-time.
I loved her casual stories about appearance, etiquette --
the way she took for granted that anyone could improve her appearance
with a little planning and concentration.

> "Take Marilyn Monroe for example.
> Terrible smile at first!
> She had to learn about presenting herself before she was so pretty and sexy.
> But she's too much. That voice!
> You want to sound more natural,
> not too loud, but not so breathy either."

My mother lowered her eyelids a bit and breathed out a line or two from the dead
President's Happy Birthday song, imitating Marilyn.
We laughed and I imitated as well.
We laughed some more.

> "Marilyn had to learn to roll her lips up around her teeth into a smile
> so they'd cover them. Like this."

She demonstrated pressing her lips firmly onto her teeth,
then peeling them back into a smile slowly
so they stayed flat against the teeth.
It didn't look quite happy,
until she added laughing happy eyes.

So much goes into a smile, I thought.
And I pitied Marilyn her diligence.

If that's just the smile,
how much concentration must go into the rest?
The voice, the walk, the sitting, standing,
small movements of her hands,
turn of her body at the waist.

How much planning would that take
to make it all look natural for her?
I wondered as I drifted to sleep in my childhood bed.

Of course, my mother knew the truth.
Appearing naturally beautiful could be taught and learned
the knowledge bought and sold.
And that after a while, the new habits do become natural
just the way you are.
So it was for Marilyn, I'm sure.

But with that knowledge, that she had been so coached,
my mother was jaded.
None of that was natural, couldn't everyone tell?
The trick was in planning to look "natural."
And this is what I learned, in my childhood.
Make-up to enhance the structure of the face, not embellish it.
Clothing to hide what were called "figure flaws"
not draw undue attention to either hips, bust or legs.
A well modulated voice, presenting refined diction, naturally.
All of it contrived to bring out the "natural" beauty of the woman.

But what of the nature of the flawed figure -- the loud voice?
I wondered this through years of non-conformity.
I wondered where nature resides, if not in these hips, thighs and breasts
when all we do is somehow constructed for viewing by another.
And really, we just make it "look natural."
I am thankful now that the body does not always conform,
refuses to look natural as it is being pinched or cut.
But then, my eye's view is still outside the norm.

They sold Marilyn's pots and pans.
Thirty-five years after her death,
the intimate contents of her household on the auction block.
The mundane aspects of her life,
kitchen items, driver's license, ashtrays,

dog-eared copies of her favorite books.
The things that betrayed her "natural" life.

Would anyone have cared if her natural life were all there was?
Would it have been so unbearably voyeuristic to think of her,
with this pan,
standing by a stove
wearing a terry cloth robe
cooking soup for dinner?
Or to imagine her sore and sweating foot
emerging from the Ferragamo pump
that you now hold.
Fondling a book that seems to prove
she did read, and think,
as she turned her head, just so,
cast her eyes, down at just a 35 degree angle.

Capra Lybica

Puma Perl

CHLOE'S ASS

(with a big thanks to Courtney Love)

Chloe flips her blue plaid schoolgirl skirt into the air
Big Mike snaps at her perfect round ass,
Mary's full gorgeous breasts, Rosabella's shilouette,
and me
and me
and me,

and me, I am forever orange. Russian legs planted
on Aida's shag rug as coca leggy Latina sisters
carve pork roast, race like happy colts
to la cucina for cerveza, guava paste, cigarettes

I was cute before I left home, now,
cheek to cheek with rock goddesses,
my skin folds, Chloe calls me Mommy,
I zip camera case into motorcycle leather,
bus ride through Chinatown, pearls
roll under our feet, slip through our fingers,
discolored by regret and lemon juices,

I still walk fast and think faster,
my eyes tell stories you can't understand,
Karma calls your name at midnight,
pray to your Gods, not mine,
shoot contrition into collapsed veins
recite poems to a lonely doorman,
betrayal laced with cum shots and pussy
opens like a broken umbrella, spokes
chipped and snarling, and me, and me,

I am forever orange, telling stories
you won't understand, Karma's
waiting under violet streetlights,
go on, take everything…
take everything…
take everything…

Puma Perl

EMBRACE IT!

PUMA: Oh my God! Look at me in that video! I look one hundred years old! I'm like an old lady in punk rock clothes!
(SOB SOB SOB)

BIG MIKE: Well, not all of us can be Elle McPherson.

PUMA: What??? I'm literally ready to curl up and die and that's your response? "Well, you're no Elle McPherson?"

BIG MIKE: I didn't say Well, you're no Elle McPherson. I said Not all of us can BE Elle McPherson. Elle McPherson is Elle McPherson. You're you. Look how happy you look in that shot. Can't you focus on that?

PUMA: Either happy or it's a sign of impending senility. Is that my walker leaning on the wall behind me?

BIG MIKE: Everyone gets older. Embrace it.

PUMA: Embrace it???

BIG MIKE: EMBRACE IT!!!!!

PUMA: You yelling at me?

BIG MIKE: NO! I mean….no, of course not.

PUMA: I think you were yelling at me. Embrace it! Embrace this! (GRABS CROTCH!)

BIG MIKE: You're finally coming to your senses. Anyway, what's the alternative?

PUMA: I guess there is none.

BIG MIKE: You can still take your clothes off. No one will object, except the self-appointed belly dancing, Indian food eating censors. Is there anyone here who objects?
(PROVOKE AUDIENCE RESPONSE)

PUMA: I am now handing Big Mike the scissors and his next actions will be at his own discretion. And we all know he has none.

BIG MIKE: She is freely and consciously handing me the scissors. I have no discretion.

PUMA: Wait! They need to know that there is no point to this performance whatsoever.

BIG MIKE (TO AUDIENCE): There is no point to this whatsoever. Can I please have the scissors?

PUMA: First, tell them I used to be hot. Tell them!!!!!

Big MIKE: She was hot! Give me the scissors!

PUMA (HANDS HIM THE SCISSORS. HE CUTS CLOTHES): Really hot! Tell them I was really hot!

BIG MIKE: She was really, really hot!

PUMA: I have pictures!!!!!!

BIG MIKE: So do I! Polaroids!!!!

PUMA: There is absolutely no socially redeeming value to any possible nudity in this performance.

BIG MIKE: We are socially unredeemable.

PUMA: I have no self-acceptance whatsoever, and Big Mike just likes to get women's clothes off any way he can.

BIG MIKE: YEAH! Take it off!

PUMA: I have no belief that everyone is beautiful and I think people should be shot when they're no longer hot.

BIG MIKE: Shoot them! Shoot all the old, non-hot people!

PUMA: This is not integral to any script or plot and makes no sense at all.

BIG MIKE: No sense at all!!!!

PUMA: It means nothing!

BIG MIKE: Nothing! No value! No logic! We're meaningless!

PUMA: We're the Seinfelds of performance art.

BIG MIKE: Nice tits, Elaine.

PUMA: Thank you. I forgot why we even did this.

BIG MIKE: No reason whatsoever!

PUMA: Perfect! In a naked, DaDa sort of way!

BIG MIKE: Naked, DaDa, YEAH!

Stephanie Feuer

THE TOPOGRAPHY OF ME

My arm has a topography all its own, a map of suffering rendered in flesh. Souvenir of a morning like any other; breakfast in the blue plaid bell-sleeved shirt, soft like a baby's bunting, I leaned in to smell fresh ground beans in the cone of the Melita pot on the gas range. The tiny kitchen filled with a putrid smell, my thoughts still dull before coffee, the smell of burning hair, burning flesh.
Mine.
Impossible.
Pain spread fast, flames no longer undeniable, rising up, cherry red, to gobble a near finished article on the kitchen counter. I slapped down the white hot dancing flame with my hand, it licked at my face, my breast. The green blanket on my futon on the floor my salvation. Stop Drop Roll, remembered. Order of operations; save my face, save my breast. Immolation. My arm, the sacrifice, as flame ate through to muscle. Bones can scream.
A prayer to die fast, then I willed myself not to pass out. I changed my shirt, a skein of skin slides off my arm.

My arm has a topography all its own, landscape exposed, surfaces refigured. Cold metal on my rear, a strip of skin peeled off like a potato, then harvested to grow in the crater in my arm. There is no healing for the crater in my soul, unable to do anything for myself but the debridement, the removal of dead skin. Forever changed.
My body cries out for cover.
Searing pain, a body remembers.
After skins grafts and sensation dulled by morphine drips, my skin tight and itchy, my arm resplendent with angry red scars, fibrous and inflamed.
Ugly.
Always the choice of what to reveal. A new man, lights out, shirt on. Slowly peeling back the layers, forever changed. Touch is different, having known fire, insatiable. The contours of love altered by the quenchless tongues of flame.

My arm has a topography all its own, a heart shaped scar, a map of change, rendered in flesh. Little raised lines of brown flesh, mountains of will. White pockets like lakes, the depth of pain unfathomable.
Years later, little black dress, a prim blonde stares, no beauty in what I expose. A muscle marred, a map of recovery, of choice of life, hot and fierce.

My arm has a topography all its own, rendered in flesh
 a heart shaped scar,
permission to not be perfect.

Sandra Ramos O'Briant

MIRROR MIRROR

My mother told me I was beautiful. She was always saying stuff like that, telling me what a gorgeous baby I was, and how I'd won a Beautiful Baby contest and had my picture printed in a calendar. January was my month. She compared me to movie stars, and in high school tried to draw me out of a nerdy adolescence by telling me that I had sex appeal, an important item in her lexicon of female virtues. She never explained how to use that gift, but encouraged me to date.

One night, we watched an old Ava Gardner movie together — The Barefoot Contessa. I sat on the end of her bed and brushed my long hair, my head tilted to the side. She must have been watching me. "Your neck is the same as Ava Gardner's," she said. I looked at Ava, seductive in a gypsy dance, and couldn't get past the cleft in her chin and the valley between her breasts.

"No, it's not," I said, more harshly than I intended.

We watched Jane Fonda in Barbarella together. "You look like Jane Fonda," she said. My hair was lighter then, and laden with curls, like Jane's.

"No, I don't," I said, and walked out of the room.

Many years later, my son was two years old and I still looked pregnant. "I'm too fat," I told my mother.

"You're beautiful," she said with conviction, and looked at me with appraising eyes from my top to my round bottom. "You look like Jacqueline Bisset, only she's too skinny."

"I do?" I said, and studied my profile in the mirror.

My son's in college now, and I still look pregnant. But I carry an image of myself that defies logic. I pass a mirror in my house, and out of the corner of my eye see a stranger. Who's that matronly woman, shoulders slouched and with a crease between her eyebrows? I stop to examine my reflection, and a slow morph occurs. Straighten the shoulders, suck in my gut, and smile, and yes, there she is. Yes, tilt my head — yes, I still have it — Ava Gardner's neck. The same.

Eleanor Gaffney

ADVICE TO WOMEN AT FORTY

Go braless to your mammogram,
loose and large and low cut.

Watch a woman exit the elevator
at Advanced Radiation Oncology.
Eye the wig.
Assume you are different.

Remember this as you are stickered,
gowned, indented, flattened.
Ignore fear.
Pinpoint love.

Obey as they call you back and press
until you gasp, a tear rolling into your hair.
Avoid the white circle
on your films.

Wait in your pink gown that barely covers.
Dodge the others across from you,
one addressed as Sister.
(Who said it was the nun's disease?)

Hold on. Silence competing
thoughts full of static.
Be magazine numb.
Then, the nod to leave.

Shake off the gown.
Reach your arms up.
Let your t-shirt enfold you.

Cross the parking lot
loose and large and low cut.

Heidi Joseph

THE FIRST WHITE HAIR

Later than her usual darkness waking time
in a line of dusty sunlight
she pulls the first white hair from her head
It curls upon itself
like a snake angry to be found
She pulls it across her bottom lip
tastes its strength
It feels
like fishing tackle
She winds it around her index finger
until the tip turns purple
She pulls until her finger nearly passes out
It stretches
does not break
I could cut clay with this hair
she thinks
I could string beads on it
One hundred more
and I could make a butterfly net

Heather Haldeman

BUTTERFLY TATTOO

"It's all set," my eighty-four year old mother said to me. "I'm getting a tattoo on September 2nd!"

It's the latest episode in our mother's colorful life. After all, this is the woman who, after her second husband left her, sold her diamond to go to Italy to find another man.

She has wanted a tattoo ever since she beat breast cancer twelve years ago. I offered to pay for it as a gift, but she never had the nerve to do it. She's collected names and cards of tattoo parlors. Told everyone that she wants one, but, up until now, it's been all talk.

She always claimed that she has a few "tattoos" from the radiation markings. "But, that's different," she told me. "I'm ready for the real thing now - a butterfly on the ankle."

"Go for it, Mom. Why wait."

"Well, my friends keep telling me that a tattoo is permanent - that I'll have it for the rest of my life. Then, I think, who are they kidding? How long can that be?"

My nephew, Jeffrey, sporting a few of his own tattoos, knew just the right place - The Shamrock Social Club. "On the good part of the Sunset Strip," Mom said. "A guy named Freddy will be doing it."

I urged her to check with her doctor. She called him right away – a sign that she was ready.

"He says it's fine, but not to get it right on the ankle. Says it will swell up if you put it too close to the bone." This was not the usual call he gets from his older patients, he added. She'd made his day.

I was prepared for her to back out when the big day arrived, but she was on board. I needed more reassurance though, and did one last check of the parlor on Yelp to find lots of five star reviews.

At three o'clock, we arrived at Shamrock joined by my son, Joseph, with his camera, my nephews, Justin and Jeffrey, and Justin's girlfriend, Maggie – all to cheer her on.

The place smelled like cigarettes, and had a large pool table in the center. The back of the shop is where the work is done. Mom seemed at home as she took a seat at the small bar in front, turning the pages of an album of Freddy's work as if it were one of her celebrity magazines.

Freddy appeared with a grey stubble, looking somewhere in his early sixties. He was wearing a dark grey fedora, a Hawaiian shirt layered over a white t-shirt and board shorts. He extended a tattooed hand to greet my mother. He'd been sketching a phoenix for her.

"I've changed my mind," she said. I held my breath. I knew it. She couldn't do it.

A pause, then, "I think I want a Monarch Butterfly."

Freddy handed her two books filled with photos, then headed to the computer to search for more butterflies, coming up with a perfect Monarch from an image on the screen.

"That's it!" Mom said. "Only a little smaller, like the size of an inch."

Freddy nodded, "Sure thing." Then, led her to his workstation.

We helped her up onto the tattoo chair. Once in position, Mom jokingly covered her eyes with her hands, the tips of her false lashes peaking out just above her long, squared-off orange acrylic nails.

It was her last chance to get out of it. "This is it, Mom."

"Sure is," she replied.

With a gloved hand, Freddy disinfected the skin above her left ankle, then, placed a stencil of the butterfly in the area. Satisfied, he turned on the tattoo gun, dipped it into a small cup of the black indelible ink and began the outline.

Tat-tat-tat-tat. "You ok, Marilyn?" Freddy asked Mom.

She replied with a slight wince. "Great."

Jeffrey leaned in. "This is the worst part, Nana," he said, "the color doesn't hurt as much."

"Is that music in the background, rap?" Mom asked. I could tell she was trying to distract herself.

Buzzing away, Freddy answered. "Nope. Punk. You like rap?"

"Not really." Mom moved on to her favorite question. "What sign are you Freddy?"

Focusing on the margins inside the wings, he replied, "Cancer."

My older son, Allan, texted me. "Stuck in LA traffic. I'm going to miss it!"

Just as Freddy began coloring the forewing orange, Jeffrey announced that Mom had nine followers on his Facebook page that "liked" that she was getting a tattoo.

My mother winced. "You alright?" I asked.

"Only hurts when I laugh." She relaxed a bit. "Childbirth is worse."

Freddy dipped the gun into the tiny cup of orange paint.

Mom peaked over to see the wings. "Did you know that orange was Sinatra's favorite color?"

Freddy smiled and wiped the tattoo with a fresh paper towel and applied a thin coat of ointment.

"Everyone of my friends is getting their faces and eyes done. I'd rather do this," she said, admiring Freddy's work. "Maybe a little diamond in the nose is next."

I rolled my eyes.

"Just kidding."

The light from my son's camera flash bounced off of the slightly tilted butterfly on Mom's ankle. It looked beautiful.

In an hour, my mother had her butterfly. Delighted, she leaned forward in the chair, pressing her hands down toward her ankles. "Look, it matches my nails!"

"How old is the oldest person you've done?" I asked him.

"Seventy-one."

Freddy gave Mom her aftercare instructions and I settled up – feeling like he had way undercharged me. "She's special," he said.

Gathering outside the shop for a group photo, Mom smiled. "No turning back now!"

She pointed her toe to the camera to show it off. "Next month I start guitar lessons."

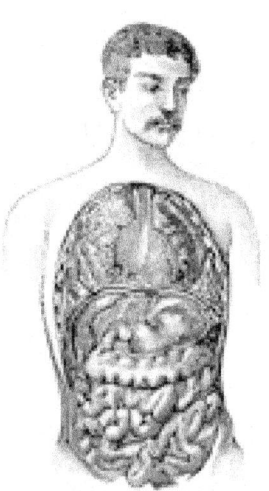

Donna Katzin

EMINENT DOMAIN

Overnight
it seems that age
has settled in,
an uninvited guest,
and taken possession
of the man I love.

Behind the weather-worn façade
the massive frame,
once powerful,
now needs repair.

Broken beams no longer bear their weight
so willingly
and pipes must be unclogged
with regularity --
the ones we can.

A quaver in the voice swings tentatively
back and forth --
a door on rusty hinges.
Erratic drafts drift
from an upstairs window
someone left open.

Outside the daisies and forget-me-nots
no longer bloom,
but in the hearth
the fire still burns.

Lois Marie Harrod

THE REAL SPINE OF THE MILKY WAY

My sister's bed: a gray tornado gathering up to Oz and down among the dwarfs and
ducks. Climb on her little wagon with the charlatans and quack we go.
She's adding cures, her latest—hand-swirl circles radiating hurricane-force energy.
The cure for Dad's forget, Mom's dental bill, Rover's sleepless
nights, just off the rant side of the meteor. As for the son-in-law
x-rating it off with the sexy radiologist, he'll never get it up
again, my sister will see to that, a simple matter, she says,
adjusting hormones to the stars, some men are much too fit
to live, soon he'll be sick as dodo, dead
as dick, and meanwhile she's raising
a prayer dome over the rest of us,
protecting us from tsunami,
dam failure and shipwreck off Somalia.
And if that doesn't work, she's tracked
down an orgone box. Doubt
is not in her vocabulary,
and she seems heaven-bent on wiping out
the species, one rat after another.
It's happened all before,
she says, karma,
and she doesn't mean
Noah's flood,
she means
annihilation
of the whole goddamn
human race,
is there
anything
we've done
that she
should
save?

Linda McCauley Freeman

I am

not the body that's left
staring at I don't know what
holding up holding back
holding on

my body's hired keeper
cleans my shit chooses
my clothes the white
sensible shoes I always hated
laced tight

my husband still
makes meatloaf with extra
onions plays the cards
fanned in my hand
I always hated cards

my firstborn gloats she is now
my favorite hides me
from all others I ever
loved her sister just tries tries
cries

and my sons my sons my wardens
prop my diminished body into
existence

none of you can see me--
I am only as I am not but I am
a person not a thing the place
you called home.

Claudia Van Gerven

NOT ALL TOGETHER

Her mind and the body do not keep
much company. They are badly
mated. The head spins off
a toy gyroscope, whirling around
itself with a contented hum. It hugs
its axis so tightly it feels weighty,
thinks of itself as quite solid and upright.
It cannot imagine its own airiness,
its involutions, the terrific speed it takes
to be always in the same place.

The body patiently wraps itself in fat cells,
lines all its drawers with old newspaper,
hordes the last strangling fruits
in its thick, damp cellar. The empty
hands grow heavy with dust of heaven.
The heart dutifully opens and closes
its gristle doors, as millenniums
rush in and out.

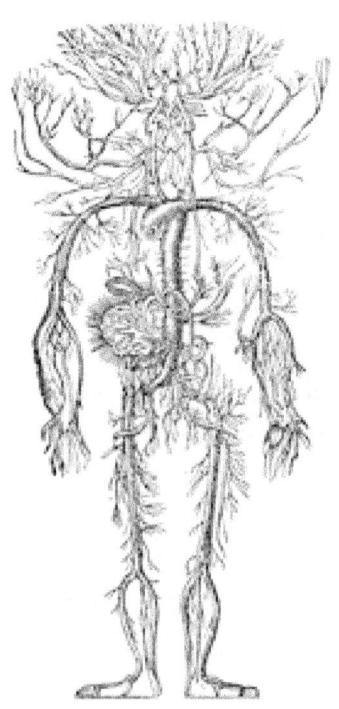

Claudia Van Gerven

SUN BONNET SUE PUSHES UP DAISIES

She loves the shape of
the grave, its vagueness,
the shifting walls. Even
the casket, with its predictable
hexagon, could not resist
the subtleties of death,
slow drift of tectonic plates,
shape-shifting of roots.
She could sense them inching
closer, those glorious angels
of change, feel them nibbling
on the eternal outline of the hat,
scalloping the immemorial brim.
She could endure anything
for the rapture of
this touch, little rootlets
fingering her unimagined
breasts, pure white grubs
tasting the sweetness of
her inner thighs. She felt
stifling calico being gnawed
away, as she surrendered seismically
to the caress of root hairs,
felt herself explode
into a hallelujah of dusty wings,
breaking irresistibly from
funeral wrappings. Mated
at last to angel of
death, she erupts
into a wilderness of daisies.

Leah Sewell

DETECTING THE CELL

Each trip to the girls' room
makes a worried woman of me.
The moon's knowing eye has changed from a sliver
to a long blink, and the cup of wine
you offer me uncertainly
smells of aluminum and blood.

Don't tell me what visions skirted across
the windshield on your drug store journey

while I swept your apartment, sashaying my hips
between the nervous moods that licked
beneath my navel. Breaking to rest,
the Surgeon General warned me
but I feigned ignorance, and the smoke
danced like a New Year's dragon,
ferocious and funny,
in the bleak southern light through the window.

Here you are with a bottle and a box,
blindfold and crystal ball.
I gulp the sludge defiantly and it coats me
like realization of a dreadful mistake.
The trip to the girls' room
makes a worried woman of me.

Therese Gilardi

SANCTUARY CITY

Blood volume builds
The red army mounts
lifeless
in a saline solution.

Folic acid in hand
My fat fingers reach
for the bump battleground.

Prepped and primed for deliverance
from dark mortal wounds
on a gunmetal gurney
that tastes of moon dust.

My open womb empty
A spent treasure chest
toy soldiers afloat
in a sea of dead dolls.

It's my fault
The general
with no battle plan
My sanctuary city
whose walls I let breech.

Susan Rukeyser

OUR BLOODY SECRETS

I remember how it was. Every month, the blood. Usually met with indifference, occasionally relief. For women, just the way it is. We don't talk about it much, but blood unites us.

I remember how it was, when I was pregnant. I was older this time, my son already eight and eager for a sibling. (With him, I bloomed with happy pregnancy. I delivered without drugs. I felt invincible. I thought, I should do this for other women. Be a surrogate for those who want babies but month after month see nothing but blood.)

I remember how it was, when blood came when it shouldn't. In week ten, the embryo becomes a fetus. It looks like a comma: big head, a curve of body. Just over an inch long, the size of a kumquat. If it's wished-for, it's a baby.

First, just a hint. Then undeniable pink. Loathsome red. I staggered to the bathroom, all of me pouring out.

I lowered myself to tile, afraid of how much would come. I affixed one pad to another. I scrubbed at a drop on my sock, making it worse.

"By the time you see blood it's too late," a nurse later told me.

My son, the child who lived, grew from kumquat to avocado to butternut squash. Then he slipped from me, not a day too soon, ready for the world.

One morning before Kindergarten, we buried his tadpole in a grassy hill behind our house. His baby frog, dead too soon. It dissolved into dirt, reduced to fluid and thin tissue that clung to the surface. Some life isn't meant to last.

We called the doctor's office; the nurse said to come in. She emphasized: "This happens more often than people realize." Women are united by their secrets, too.

"You may need a D&C," she said. "There's a risk of infection, serious bleeding."

I winced at "serious."

"You'll need a shot, if you're Rh negative, and the baby was—"

"Was?" I asked, but she pretended not to hear.

In the doctor's waiting room, I was surrounded by bellies swollen with success. Beige walls pressed in, reflecting too much light. I was bent with surging waves of pain like labor, or almost. My husband asked the receptionist, again, if I could wait somewhere else. He was told, again: No. Mothers-to-be glanced sideways at my sweatpants, my puffy eyes and unbrushed hair. They knew. I was humiliated, but sorry, too, for the bad omen I was. Don't look, I whispered into patterned carpet.

"Deceased for days, probably," announced the doctor. My body, bare and empty, shivered beneath a paper gown. He said I should've brought the expelled material. Sometimes it offers an explanation. They run tests. I didn't have anything to give him, but if I did I wouldn't tell.

Back home, I avoided the bathroom. My grief lived in the grout between tiles, in the toilet. I should have thrust my fingers into blood, in case there was something to retrieve. I should have tried to find something to bury in dirt, like the tadpole reduced to fluid and thin tissue.

For days life drained from me. I collapsed to soggy rubble. "What kind of a mother?" I whispered, too many times. My eight year old didn't know. He went to school. My husband went to work. They went out amongst the living. I was glad to be spared my son's questions. I had no answers, only guilt.

Choice is power, I've always believed this. Free women choose to accept or deny lovers, to welcome children, or delay them, or refuse them. As I lay in bed, still in sweatpants and layers of pads, I wondered if losing this tiny fetal comma—to me, my baby—would weaken this conviction. My thoughts tumbled: Is it punishment? I'd never believed in a vengeful God, but I fretted: Because all those years I considered a fetus a collection of viable cells, not a baby? Perhaps that's why?

I wanted this blame, but I couldn't convince myself. I didn't believe it anymore than I believed a ten week old fetus was really a baby, for any reason besides our love for it. For him, or her.

Miscarriage didn't turn me against choice. I was relieved when I realized this. The blood didn't wash all of me away. Although it did humble me. I was never invincible. What was lost wasn't a comma, or a kumquat, or a fetus. Loved already, it was our child.

Now I know a woman's power results from choice but also voice: speaking aloud our bloody secrets.

Afterwards, when the monthly blood arrived on schedule, I was not indifferent. Not relieved. How long would all blood remind me of that blood? How long would my shame keep me silent? Too long.

A woman's body may betray her, lose its hold on a wanted child. Likewise, it may implant an egg fertilized by someone she doesn't love, someone uninterested in parenthood. Someone bad. The betrayal goes both ways.

Some life isn't meant to last. Every month, another bloody reminder.

Donna Coffey

THE CUT

By the time Bethany decides she wants the epidural,
it's too late. Her grandmother flees her screams.
I stay, stroke and kiss her sweating face,
watch her push until a slick black head crests.
I see the slippery red infant slide into the midwife's hands.
We both hear the first cry.

Their umbilical cord glistens like a jelly fish
and spirals like an old telephone cord.
The midwife hands me scissors.
I cut the cord like a priest kills a dove,
          feeding blood to a thirsty God.
The nurse washes the screaming baby,
wraps her in a blanket, plants her in my arms,
guides me away from Bethany like a funeral director
ushering out the mourner who can't stop stroking
          a dead boy's hair.

Bethany's grandmother and I stand in front of the glass wall,
watch newborns squirm in bassinets.
I said I wouldn't look at her, but I'm looking, she says.
You have to, I tell her,
          as if I know a thing about it.

Bethany is in one hospital room, my husband and I in another.
The baby is wheeled between the rooms,
and I'm not sure who I'm rooting for.
Bethany leaves in a wheelchair.
Her shoulders humped
like an old woman's.
Her grief is in her neck.
Her eyes flat and dry
          as I bend to kiss her forehead.

The night nurse says we can't take the baby home.
No matching armband.
She calls Bethany to make her bring it back.

It's her eighteenth birthday. I move in close to the nurse's
smug face, want to slap her, could easily kill her.
She squeaks along the corridors in those soft-soled shoes,
ferreting out grief in the small square rooms.
        It's not hard to find.

I picture Bethany in her kitchen.
The neat slice
through the white plastic cuff.
The scissors at her wrist.
As a butcher holds a chicken by the neck.
        Snips with shears that cut through bone.

Amanda Regan Lighthiser

HONEYSUCKLE JUICE

Nine months ago we lit up. My son brightened in my belly; your tumor radiated
heat. Me, full of movement, marveling at my body's capabilities while yours waged
a bitter betrayal.

I felt so far from you, my girlhood friend. You, who spent hours plucking honeysuckles in my backyard. How many white blossoms did we squeeze, for only an
ounce of juice?

Now you and my boy share a fine newness; sparse and softly flaxen, here and
there—

I touch my lips to that tender spot, still open.

Here is where we can find one another. This is how we are born again.

T.T. Jax

SOLIDARITY

We work together: you explain the procedure, smiling, guide her to lifting spreading as you sufficiently supply the straps. The anesthesiologist slips a needle into her vein: asleep. The doctor, then, lifts a sterile
instrument gleaming in fluorescent light and inserts it (in the slim face of steel we are all reflected: mercurial, distorted, pulled across the surface as it moves): the woman on the table jumps. Tuesdays, Fridays, and Saturday afternoons, we flip a switch. Suck, gurgle: aspirated. Saturday mornings it's more complicated-- tug, pull, twist, scrape: "gently emptied," space restored to the womb. Something hotly contested in name and meaning dies, if it wasn't dead already. Through a steel window we pass the small body packaged in paper or glass. We lift the woman like she is nothing, still bleeding, jaw slack in sleep as her head sways gently on the rolling gurney. You stay to scrub the blood from the wall.

One room over, the sink is full. *There's a fucking eye clogging the drain!,* she says, as she passes instruments wet with what looks like semen or milk to me through another steel window. She counts phalanges, sorts a spinal chord, ear, elbow from a puzzle of parts. Nothing can be left inside the woman who now shivers in a recovery bed, shifting as she stares with a headless animal cracker in her fist.

A nurse comes in, paints the bottom of a foot with ink, presses it to an index card. The woman has requested this, to remember 6 months of internal stirrings she could not sustain. A footprint in ink: proof of passing, of what flashed unseen through steel windows while she slept.

In the third room I wrap instruments in birthday packages of blue paper, slip them into a hot mouth of steel and steam for cleansing. The door of the autoclave pops like a snapping clavicle as I seal it shut. Across the window plastic crackles; she double packages the necessary kill in sealed red bags. Later someone will take it, with many others, to burn to ash. For now she stores it in a box marked hazardous in red block letters.

There is no smell on earth like this: cardboard, latex, steel, steam, blood, shit, pungent chemicals specially formulated to dissolve organic matter, sharp like splinters to the nose. Burning paper, coffee grounds, clean bleached cotton linen. And their bodies: secret interstitial spaces split, cavities within cavities lined with tissue torn open to the world for the first time, split to reveal fresh fluids and pockets of gas releasing a pungent first breath never drawn. This death smells sharp and new, like cat breath; the pathology room air tastes like a belly full of yeast rising on only three hours of sleep. This smell clings to us, our skin, our hair; we eat with it, laugh with it, wear it in our teeth as we smile.

We leave when it's dark, unfamiliar in our street clothes. None of us have died today, and the purple and black ribbons pinned to our shirts are light in their reminder that this is not inconsequential. The hill we walk down is steep, pocked with shadow in street light. A guard sees us safely to our cars. I drive slowly, chainsmoking contraband menthols as the road unravels to home. When I open the door my daughter rushes to hug me; I am unprepared for the brush of her cheek on mine, her quick and insistent pulse. She wishes me to hold a rock she found, but my palm is full of a woman's tears.

Martha Kinkade

MORPHINE

Ominous and fixed, the clock hands surround the number 12: wide, big, and hovering over the hospital bed and dripping down toward my feet. My vision holds the thin black hands cupped in a saucer. The nurse slides across my periphery, she's crying; she's hugging me. Death has walked in and I'm given morphine.

I see the green mask before I recognize the doctor. I feel stagnant. He breeches my awareness like an elixir with jumbled words. I hear, the baby's dead…no chance of living…cyclopia and then, my clock's eye: ticking, ticking, ticking.

And 5 minute doses, morphine.

Mother rubs my feet and my hand disappears. I tell myself I should feel warmth, but I don't. Shivering turns to shaking. Time isn't moving as waves and waves swallow any sense of time continuum, for it has stopped. Yet every 5 minutes, morphine. They come in. They say, see the baby. They say, sleep. They say, try and see the baby. They bring pictures of her frozen body with white chalk welded over her tiny frame. A skullcap covers her face and draws my eyes to her pink lips, plump as if freshly kissed.

They remove the staples from my loose belly. I recognize a cut. I recognize anger. I'm cut open with resentment for not having my child there, alive. When they bring her in, a Polaroid follows. I'm hollow as she's unwrapped. Her petite, well-formed fingers, feel like mine, only cold. Her eye, a black circle reflects a depth that bares creation; it's creased on both sides. And I mourn for what might have been. I pose with a slight smile for memory picture. As I look at my daughter again, I see a clock without hands. Her skin frayed with pale spider lines that fracture her frozen skin. I am a good mother; I tell myself this as I hold my deformed and dead child. She'll be cremated, but first they'll cut her frail sternum, call her a specimen and find holes as they search her heart.

I hate morphine. Its numbness wears off, and the pain in my heart aches as I breathe.

Laura A. Ciraolo

EMILY DICKINSON SPEAKS
TO SYLVIA PLATH ABOUT METAPHORS

It is the full moon
and I feel the loss
of my purse the most,
the tug of its straps,
the weight on my belly,
haunting sensations, a missing limb.
At the ebb tide, apparently,
it turned into wizened leather,
empty, scraped, worn and useless,
latch, buckles, broken or missing.
Best to throw it out—
there's nothing to carry anyway.

Cynthia Veach

ON THE EVE OF YOUR MASTECTOMY

If breasts were pears they would break
into blossom with reckless abandon
and grow flush, nubile buds
on the slenderest of limbs.
Overnight, the fruit would take shape,
rising effortlessly as bread rises
doubling and redoubling
so every branch became an offering of plump flesh.
If breasts were pears we would take them into our mouths,
nuzzle the pith with our tongues,
and suckle until the juice
ran in sticky rivulets down our chests.

Theta Pavis

THINKING OF SUSAN AT THE FOLLOW-UP

On the black film
the picture of my breast
looks like the moon
before men landed there.

The doctor's white hands
hold the rectangle
up to the light.
She's touching the map of me.

I'm staring at the breast-crusher
in the corner, wondering who
decided to name it Selena?

What if you came here and
your name was Selena?

Or what if your cousin died
when you were just a girl
and you were there, at the edge
of her bed when it happened.

Would you stand over
the heating vent in the floor
the next morning,
watching your nightgown poof out
from the forced air?

What if the Vermont winter was
so cold the icicles outside were
as long as spears?

What if your cousin died on
her birthday? And your father
didn't know what to do with the
red wool blanket he'd brought
for a present.

So he gave it to you

Fay Chiang

LANDMARKS AND GEOGRAPHY

I Cut. June.1994. Lumpectomy. 3 tumors the size of marbles from the right breast.

   Cut. August. 1994. Quandrantectomy. One quarter of the right breast.
   Cut. November. 1994. Mastectomy. Right breast.
   Cut. June. 1997. Axillary Lymph Node Dissection. 3 lymph nodes right armpit.
   Cut. October. 2003. Hysterectomy. 20 pound fibroid.
   Cut. October. 2003. Oophorectomy. Both ovaries.
   Cut. December. 2004. Lobectomy. Right lung. Lower lobe. Fist-sized tumor.
   Cut. December. 2004. Bone biopsy of right lower rib. No metastisis.
   Cut. September. 2010. Pneumothorax. Right lung collapsed.

   and oh,

Cut. July. 1979. Appendectomy. Burst appendix.
Cut. August. 1989. Birth of my daughter. 47 hour labor.

This body held together by
so many stitches and scars---
these are the landmarks and geography
in the journey of a life.
my life.

II Know that I rejoice
   still standing
     despite 3 tumors still in the right lung
     despite sciatica's pain coursing from spine to toe
     despite pain from scars and phantom body parts
   still walking
     all hours of the night and day
     the streets and canyons of this city
      of my birth
     Chinatown, the Lower East Side,
      and East Village my home
     wind, sun, rain, snow and sleet---
      elements against my open face
   still alive.

III   Entering my 6th decade
       I see hikes in all 7 continents
         re-visiting Italy, Mexico, South Africa,
       Europe, Asia; venturing to new places
         in North America, South America,
        Australia, Africa

      and for the first time,
        home to my father's village,
          in Muy Kwok, SunWei,
   Guangdong, China.

      My cousin tells me,
        10,000 Chiangs once lived
       on fertile farmland
          ringed by mountains and virgin forest
         a river running through it
           flowing towards the sea

     The house our great-grandfather built
       stands behind stonewalls;
       a gate opens to a kitchen garden and
         a pink house
         built by the government
          in exchange for using
           our ancestral lands

       Yes, I will stay in The Pink House
         calling home
the landmarks and geography
in the journey of a life.
my life.

Lacertus aquaticus   *Lacertus Viridis*

Nancy Cook

CLOSE TO THE HEART

I am planning the perfect tattoo. Where to have it applied is not in question: It is going to cover my entire chest. But beyond that, I have some decisions to make.

My relationship with my breasts has always been complicated. So much different than Joel's relationship with his penis. Joel's penis has a name. The penis is named Max, basic and simple. Max has a personality, so Joel believes, a life of its own, completely separate from Joel's. Well, not completely separate, of course. Our son Aaron views his little penis in much the same way. Aaron thinks his penis is his friend, although he hasn't given it (him?) a name. Joel is convinced this is evidence of relational capacity. I say if you are in conversation with a body part, addressing it as Other, that's distancing, not intimacy. But to be candid, I don't care enough to get into a real discussion about it.

It's strange to me because my breasts have always been part of the integrated whole that is my body. This was true even before I had real breasts, when I was a kid pushing my flat chest up and out so I could look like my Mom or Charlie's Angels or Madonna. I'd check out my reflection in a mirror or a sun-glared store window, and there they'd be, future boobs, more real than imaginary. It's like my body always knew breasts would be part of the family, and now they're participants in a full-fledged collaboration, right in there with my ears, my toes, my heart. My body parts communicate pretty well, the soles to the brain, the nostrils to the spine, the nipples on direct-dial to the vulva. My breasts are as essential as, and no more essential than, other parts, say, my tongue or my hands.

At the same time, I've often felt as if these beauties were not mine alone. They're so, you know, out there. Visible. Available for public notice. Something like marigolds in a house-front flower bed or news of winning even a minor prize. Joel would probably take issue with that. He likes that he has private viewings. He coos, he tastes. Sometimes he plays them, left side against the right. He might grasp tightly, squeeze hard, but never roughly. I understand Joel's attraction to my breasts, if not his proprietariness. I like personal time with my breasts too. They are nice to touch and very responsive. Especially when an effort is made.

Not that I've had much private time with my breasts in recent years. Aaron made his claim on them as a baby, then the girls, Emma and Josie, had their turns. And, most recently, the doctors. I suspect that Joel has not liked any of this, although he's too nice a guy to complain.

But back to the big question: what is the perfect tattoo? What will pay tribute to feminine beauty, strength, sensuality? Motherhood. Solidarity and survival. I could go with a Xena the Warrior, the whole Amazonish thing. I've considered an artful rendition of a dinner feast, grander than Thanksgiving, smoky and steamy meats, a colorful overabundance of shining fruits and bloated roots and huge leafy sprays, a mountain of fresh bread loaves, luscious pies and puddings and creamed pastry puffs. Or maybe a circle dance, women of every size and shade with hands joined. Then, with every twist of shoulders, the women's bare feet would boogie, their heads would float musically.

One inspiration, an early morning rumination, involves whales. When I was pregnant with Aaron, Joel and I took a whale watching cruise. I'd been warned against it, the risk of nausea being so unacceptably high. But the threat of an emotional breakdown if I were denied this outing convinced both Joel and the cruise hosts that a little boat vomit was the lesser of two perils. It was a good decision. The ocean was my friend that day. I never did get nauseous and the whales surrounded our boat not once, but three times. Their glossy bodies parted the waves, rose skyward, dashed below, made showers of foam. It was early summer and young black calves by the dozen alternately clung to mothers' hides and flashed fins above the sea's swells in bold proclamations of self-reliance. With every orca sighting, unborn Aaron danced and applauded in the womb.

What I keep coming back to, though, is a profusion of roses. Roses, fragile and impermanent. Roses, red and amorous and daring, their thorny stems hidden but still there, close to the heart. Roses and roses and roses and roses, every single one's complex delicate exacting lines traceable with a fingernail. Generous gardens of roses that will take a lifetime to explore. Wild spring and summer roses, wall-climbing roses, Molly Bloom yes I will yes roses. Roses spread all across my empty chest, a gift to be bestowed after the medical healing, after the chemo and radiation are done. A gift to myself. A gift that is myself.

Patricia Thomas

ENJOYING SMOKING

My mother, a green-eyed beauty from the South, got pregnant in high school and got married, at age 19. That's what women did in the 1950's. She became a wife and mother (of me), making the switch from going to dances in pretty pastel-colored dresses, to cleaning house and changing dirty diapers without missing a beat. She started smoking cigarettes in high school (Winston's were her brand) and didn't stop until she developed emphysema 30 years later. I, along with my sister, constantly nagged her about her bad habit. For years, I clipped "Dear Abby" letters from bereaved family members of smokers and articles on the hazards of smoking and sent them to her. I doubt she ever read them.

"I enjoy smoking," she would respond, drawing out every single syllable with her wonderful Southern drawl, when anyone mentioned the possible effect of smoking on her health. She made it sound as though that was a justification. And so our pattern (my nagging and her dismissing) continued throughout the years.
She loved old romance movies, like *An Affair to Remember* and adored Katherine Hepburn. She drank cup after cup of coffee all day every day and constantly had a cigarette in her hand. One of my earliest memories is of her sitting in her overstuffed green chair in a haze of smoke, with an overflowing ashtray of cigarette butts by her side. She tended to speak in exclamatory phrases, such as "No! You don't mean it? Really? I can't believe that!" She made everything sound extraordinary.

She was a fantastic cook and never used a recipe in her life. Southern dishes were her specialty—fried chicken, chicken and dumplings, biscuits, and apple pies. If it was Southern, she could make it and she loved to eat it too, never being a "salad" kind of girl. She was a tall, strong, well-coiffed woman who never complained, not when my father left her for another woman, and not even when she reached the point of not being able to breathe without an oxygen tank.

She loved laughing and talking with her friends, most of whom she had met in high school and who she remained friends with until the day she died. When they lived in the same town, they all got together and played bridge. Most of them smoked too. After we moved to northern Alabama, away from her hometown of Dothan and her friends, she talked to them all on a regular basis for hours at a time on the phone, all the while smoking and drinking coffee. They shared stories about their husbands and children, and later the pains of growing older, and in my mother's case, becoming ill. They found something to laugh about in every conversation.

To the end my mother maintained her up-beat attitude, and amazingly never took responsibility for the effects smoking had on her life. She finally stopped smoking entirely when she could not breathe without gasping for air. She quit cold turkey, but the damage was done. The changes came gradually. At first she could not walk without effort, and then she could not ride her exercise bike. At one point she could not wash her hair without difficulty and could barely make a trip to the market for food. Eventually she became house-bound.

When she was first diagnosed with emphysema by her doctor, she innocently asked what caused it. When he replied that it was most likely a result of smoking, she replied, "But it could have been something else, couldn't it? You really don't know that it was from smoking. Right?"

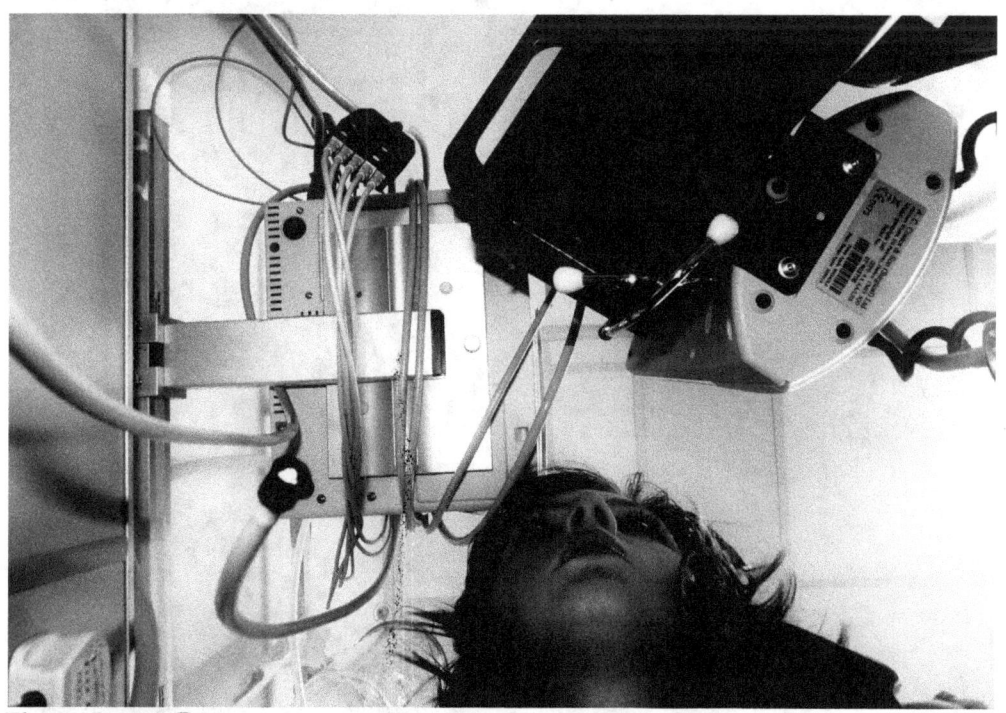

Eleanor Leonne Bennett

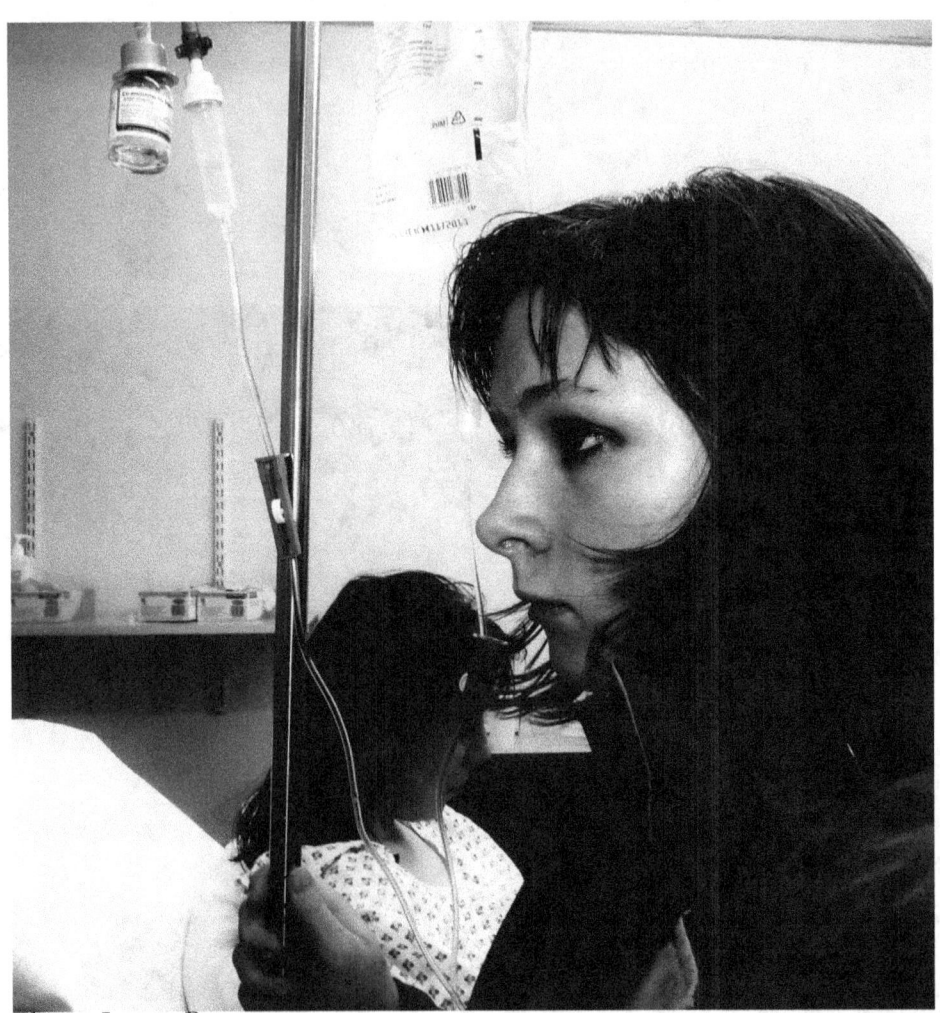

Eleanor Leonne Bennett

Evelyn Krampf

MOMMY SHRINKS

When I was seventeen, my mom stopped eating.

"After you haven't done it for a while, you just stop noticing. It's just not something you do."

She was drinking fizzy water while my brother and I ate boiled tortellini.

"This is it. This is going to change my life," she said, beaming like a porcelain doll.

I have to admit, I didn't argue with her about it at the time. It had been a long time coming. When I was little, in moments of frustration she would mutter, "I am going to lose all this weight. One of these days I am just going to burn it off."

I was highly disturbed. What did it mean that my mother was going to burn off her fat? I was really worried that one day I would see her as the person I knew — portly but not obese, curly red hair, elegant cheekbones — and watch her disappear behind the bedroom door. We would slowly catch the scent of burning flesh. She would emerge charred and sizzling, smeared with black dripping fat, a large chunk of her side gone.

"Look kids! I lost the weight!" she would say.

Actually, she seemed basically the same at first. She drank fizzy water, she drove me everywhere, she walked the dogs. She seemed rather determinedly happy. And she lost weight. Very rapidly. She shrunk, kind of shrivelled actually, so that the flesh that had loved her chin deflated and hung from the front of her neck.

In rude defiance, I learned how to cook. I did not push her to eat, because I had for years. Every year. The Atkins diet, the South Beach diet, the Ephedrin phase. Every night over the dining room table, we argued about food and eating. I would tell her to eat like a normal person. She would tell me that I had no idea what it was like to live in an aging, fat body, in order to finish the argument.

But my cooking was a different story. This was like a direct assault on everything she was struggling for. I started with lentil soup, something I knew she liked — warm, homey, low-calorie. But fascination caught on and I learned to make a variety of things over that year — canoli, stuffed zucchini, layered cakes, enchiladas. My mom at first ignored me and continued to flip through catalogues while I simmered and baked. Eventually she became passive aggressive, and then down-right hostile.

"If you insist on making a huge mess, you have to clean it up," she'd snap and storm to her bedroom, slamming the door behind her.

It's not as if she didn't know what I was doing.

The not eating thing, you would think, would be the most cost-effective diet ever. But it wasn't. It was very expensive. You couldn't just not eat by yourself, you had to go to a class to teach you how to not eat. And you had to see a special doctor once a week who would weigh you and check your blood pressure. All that stuff cost hundreds of dollars. It was not cheap to skip all that food.

As the months wore on and my mom got smaller, she talked. She had always been chatty, but with the loss of nutrition it was as if she were deflating like a basketball and all these words were hissing out. She talked about her marriage, my brother's problems with school, her menopause, her childhood poverty, her anger and her fears. As we circled around town, she slowly narrowed in on a central topic—dinner in her family home. Her father demanded that she eat every speck of food on her plate each night. There was no room for waste. During one of our longer drives she told me about the time she refused. In a moment he was behind her, his fingers wrapped around her neck. He held her this way until she licked the plate clean while she wept. I watched my mother grip the steering wheel as she spoke, her eyes wide with memory. I began cooking when she wasn't home.

Diane Raptosh

LINEAGE

The matter before us is my mother.
Her mind, embryo pendent in water.

The slope of the riverbank
we used to maunder. Among

some things the body can't remember:
Matter and *mother* burst from the baby-talk

ma, which suckling uproar also birthed
metropolis. Bridgehead and truss. The flat-

topped ziggurats. *Matter,* O mighty cloth.
Mom, the hard timber used within

carpentry. *Mama* as groundmass and muck.
Materiel and cereal crop. This is

the farmer sowing her corn that worried
the cat that lay in the house. This is the line

that helps keeps things level. Listen, Ma, I am
skittering out of my head, backsliding off the plank of the earth

Tsaurah Litzky

MY MOTHER'S BODY

If my mother was a tree, she would be a mountain evergreen
fine in the sun but flourishing also in shade or shadow,
she was tough, deep rooted in rich earth
she was unselfish, never talked about her troubles,
was virtuous in all things
unlike me.

When I was little I was fascinated by her body,
when we showered together,
I couldn't keep my eyes off her.
She had bumps on her chest,
she called them breasts
and a dark wiry patch of hair between
her legs that looked like the steel wool
she used to scour our pots,
when she washed between her legs
I could see a pink crack, I asked her what it was,
she said it was a lily,
she called the crack between my legs a lily too,
she told me one day I would have breasts and a patch,
I didn't want my mother to think I doubted her
but I wondered how such things could happen.
Now I know.

My mother is dead thirteen years,
if I could tell you how much I miss her
it would take more words then I own,
she was ivory, alabaster, tinted with rose,
her skin silk all over, her intentions gold,
she was the summer of my childhood,
she tells me stories beneath a blossoming tree,
She has given me a feathery crown that protects me,
an invisible crown that no one can see,
she is the imagination in my hands,
the bones of my feet,
a dim memory of heat.

Tsaurah Litzky

HER WHITE ARMS

In bed on nights like this,
my spirit sinking in a rough sea,
I hug myself, rock up and down,
pretend I'm inside my mother's body.

I've shot myself in the foot again,
(too many times, too much pride,
too much white wine.)

My mother never scolds,
she keeps rocking, through hurricanes,
through tsunamis, up and down,
up and down, until I feel her heat,
her white arms around me,
I forgive myself,
at least enough to sleep.

Kyle Potvin

RUBY RING

My favorite present was a ruby ring
that I inherited when Grandma died.
At 12, I was besotted by the thing.
Amazed that I was given this, I eyed
the fiery facets waving on my hand.
On Sundays, kneeling at the pew, I'd stare
into its changing depths, shifting the band
to catch the slanted light, head bowed in prayer.
One day the ring was gone. I scoured my room,
rifling through the few hiding spots I had.
For days, I'd get up early to resume
my search, afraid to tell my mom and dad.
Each time I touch my finger, rub that place,
I'm still surprised to find an empty space.

Angela S. Patane

HERE YOU ARE NOT MY MOTHER

We uncover her old photos.
I like how they have a frame:
a thin white border
smaller than a Polaroid's.

"May I have this one?"
She wants to know why.

> Because I can tell
> you're in a hotel room,
> squash yellow walls
> barely lit behind you.
> You're in a hot pink
> halter nightie—A-line,
> white stripe empire waist.
> Sideways on a rumpled bed,
> one arm drapes a pear hip,
> the other props you up.
> I can tell you tried to stick
> your knees together with sweat,
> but a white triangle is peeking.
> They must have been cotton.
> I love your pencil-thin brows,
> and your eyes lined black
> staring at whoever takes the photo—
> the bell hop, a 70s prog rock
> drummer, a bad boy biker,
> a friendless female hitchhiker
> you met at the bar downstairs?

> Here you smile without wrinkles.

"Because you were about my age."

Jessica Feder-Birnbaum

SNAP SHOTS - EIGHT YEARS OLD

She pulls her Danceskin shirt down tight.
She tries to make herself flat as a board.
She prays that the cherry bumps will disappear.
New brown and wiry hair grows down there. Gross.

*

Saturday afternoon horror movie - Creature Feature - channel 5.
One jar Planters smokehouse almonds.
Huddled in a quilt – she is snatched by warlocks.
Gasping for air, she fights for life.
Narrowly escaping she reaches for the almonds.
Jar is finished, stuffed, she's home

*

The old Uncle comes upstairs in a cloud of cigar smoke.
He says let's play a game - a dirty funny game
Everyone stares. The old Uncle wants them to take off his clothes.
She pulls off his socks. The old Uncle has smelly feet.
His toenails are yellow and cracked.
Her cousins take off his shirt.
The old Uncle is pale and hairy with a huge pot belly.
His chest is puffy like a woman's.
A gold chain hangs around his neck.
The old Uncle unzips his pants.
His underwear looks like a tight white bathing suit.
His legs are thin and hairy.
The old Uncle asks that they take off his underwear.
They shriek and back away.
She covers her eyes. But she is curious.
She peeks at the gray monster rat.
She turns away to stare out the window.
If she doesn't look, she can pretend that she didn't see

*

June dusk – air perfumed by barbeque and nearby roses.
End of season little league championship celebration.
Her brother plays short stop.
Picnic tables piled high with watermelon and macaroni salad
Cartwheel competitions on the grass.
Freeze tag. You're it until you tag someone else.
She pumps her legs on the swings - soaring into the sky.
Icy grape soda explodes into tart purple fizz.
Outside she is free.

Liz Dolan

FOR MY SISTER   1950

In the cellar was buried the dismembered body
of the cherry-cheeked child butchered by the super of 598.
And even though I thought it a myth to keep girls like me
tethered, I still hugged
the curb as I skipped by. And hugged
it even more closely on that day in June
when Daddy and our neighbor
bolted up the slate stairs to the roof bellowing,
Get the bastard, get the bastard. Pressing my flesh
against ochre stucco, I, wall-eyed,
and slack-jawed, saw your trembling five-year-old body
brindled by the ruby and magenta rays of the stairwell's
stained glass, your flaxen hair buried
in Mama's corn-flowered house coat,
the X of her arms like crossed swords guarding you.

Leslie Anne Mcilroy

WHAT'S LEFT

She knows nothing about ghosts and their thin wants,
but is haunted by the past, its hands always testing limits —
first the breast, then the nipple — resistance, shame, desire.

The fingers are real. They touch her when she's making love,
and her lover knows it. He asks her to open her eyes,
to stay here; she is already gone and can't come back,

body convulsed in some memory she can't recall,

belonging to a man who must remember the fiction
he created. He was there and so many lovers/victims
later, has forgiven himself — and her — her weakness.

He's still excited. He is still alive in the poem and takes pride
in the boldness of memory, which he's stolen from her,
but not completely. He forgot the ghosts and their thin whispers.

He forgot the body and its recall. He forgot that she can feel him
touching her, inside her, and that it won't be long before
she will speak to him in the voice of a child and he will lie

awake at night with his own apparitions. She will trail her
fingers down his chest — her lips, her blue, cold skin —
and he will die, the way men do when they've taken everything.

E.J. Antonio

some say...

i enter daylight on my terms
learn how oceans moved from a slave's mouth
to the rivers where they were bred erased and drowned

some say the ocean never moved...
the ships made it too heavy
but i carry its sandy bottom wreckage in my womb

some say the river never ran...
the drowned ones made it too heavy
but i carry water's crying and the moon in my womb

some say the ocean told me
you know your tribe by the language you cry in
steal away when nothing's left but stars

some say all the warrior women who died riding slavery's wild horses
whispered all the songs they danced to in my ear
and i will carry them in my womb forever

Debora Siegel

CHILD OF A SURVIVOR

Born to massage my mother's back
When the pain does not let her sleep
Born to know why she has that pain
To know how many months
She lay paralyzed
In an unknown bed
Infested with lice
As she hid
Born to let the past live to meet the future
Born to live another's life.

J.P. Howard

DEAR MAMA:

A Double Etheree

Dear
Mama
Please tell me
What separates
Us? What legacy
Will we leave when we leave
Each other's presence? Same smile?
Same secrets buried beneath veins?
Mama, when they bury us: no masks
Tell them no masks: let them see our scarred hearts.

Mama: let our secrets fall off the bone
Let us scrape them one by one mama
Let our mouths scream: no more whispers!
Mama can you hear my scream?
How beautiful the sound
Please mama join me
Let go this pain
This tattered
Piece of
Skin

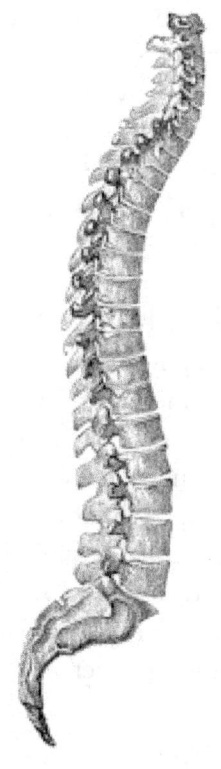

Janet Chalmers

DAVID'S "THE DEATH OF MARAT" 1793

Head turbaned in white
muslin strips soaked
with stinging vinegars,
the naked Marat sits
waist deep in an herbal bath,
his ageing shoulders
mantled in sun,
in David's painting
the papules and vesicles
of a chronically diseased skin
miraculously erased,
his face graced with
the beatific smile and
heavy-lidded eyes
of a saint or satiated lover,
in death, still a patriot
peaceful and without regret,
suffering the single
passionate thrust of
a bone-handled cutlery knife
—Christ's visible wound—
the copper soaking tub
a martyr's tomb.

Not shown:
The young noblewoman
seated in the outer foyer
ignoring the housekeeper's
screams and threats.
Marie-Anne-Charlotte
(de Corday d'Armont), a virgin
assassin from the provinces,
carrying out a mission of
revolutionary revenge,
she holds a mint lozenge
like a sacrament
on parched tongue,

her striped silk gown and
white gloves spattered
with blood, the fashionable black
hat with a feathered crown
set high on her soon to be
severed head.

John Rodriguez

SOME OLD BULLSHIT

Maasai warrior, tunic and wig of dyed red
braids, spear and sword, came to Bronx
teen program. Spoke of farming, drinking
blood from a cow, scars and broken ribs from

killing a lion. Girl poet asked
"What if I wanted to kill a lion?"
Warrior said "No, no. You are too weak.
You would take care of the children

and learn to build a house from sticks
and cow dung. You'd like it. It's very good."
Poet, worn carpenter jeans, metallic
red streak from forehead to ponytail,

arms crossed, sleeves rolled up, elbows
and knuckles scabbed from the last time
she pulled her father off her mother,
said, "Build a house? What kinda shit is that?"

Jessica Barksdale

BEDTIME STORY

As I write the words
protest, obstructing and *battery,*
a slick black raven
flaps to the lowest
limb of the half dead
cypress and begins to
pluck clean a baby robin.

If I weren't on the phone
with a legal aide,
I would be more upset.
I might think *raven murderer*
and then laugh a dark little laugh,
thinking *we need more than one raven*
to make a murder.

The aide talks on.
My son has been bused to Santa Rita jail,
where the real criminals go,
that barbed wire-protected concrete block
I used to pass by in my 1968 Volkswagen
on my way to teach English,
my two little boys and first husband
back at home reading bedtime stories.

The raven one, two, three
stabs the limp body,
feathers flying.
Even behind the window glass,
I hear the *bop bop bop*
of his hard bill as he hits
branch through flesh.
My son is in a big box jail,
visitors from eight till noon.
I write *lawyer, Tuesday,*
arraignment.

If I were outside, I'd yell and scream
until the raven flew off.
I'd sweep the feathers
from the patio. But no matter what,
the chick would still be dead.

Margo Berdeshevsky

THERE IS A RIVER FOR REVOLUTION...

At the end of the beginnings,
we dress in long light—
a hybrid body of stars—
Caress in a broken moon's lost veils,
undress, where the white owls sail.

River, where the parched heart drinks
her fill, hill where mourning can't hide,
water, where the hungering hearts call,
hill, where the unborn owlets—climb.

Winds of a sun-blind sky, call me—
shadows of streets or kisses, find me—
muses with no name, un-name me,
ghosts with no name, un-tame me, body
. . . where the unborn owlets climb . . .

There is a river for revolution,
and revolution is coming in . . .

Waters, where hungering hearts fall,
hills, where the broken wings climb . . .
seas, where the parched heart
finds her fill, hills where the old
owls climb. . . to hills where the peace
hides. . .
All pulses . . . praying . . . there's a river where
the wing tears . . . and there is a day
when the owl sails . . . and there is a river—for
revolution—the hardest love that's coming in.

Bring me to the river where lives begin,
where revolution—is coming in. . .
At the end of beginnings, souls without name,
un-name me, revolution without name—un-tame me. . .
dressed in the river's open hands: for the hard love that's coming in.

And bring me to the river where lives begin, where
our nakedness needs no skin,   bring me to the river
where it begins and begins   and a revolution is coming in . . .

Cassie Premo Steele

IN THE IMAGE OF ME

In the image of me,
red and brown and bleeding,
the world was made--
not from word, so righteous,
not from breath, so dry,
not from light, so blinding,
not from air, so high--
but shy and wet
and dark and deep
came the world--
crying, crawling,
sweet-smelling
of mud and muck--
the world arrived
in moans and sighs
from between my two strong thighs.

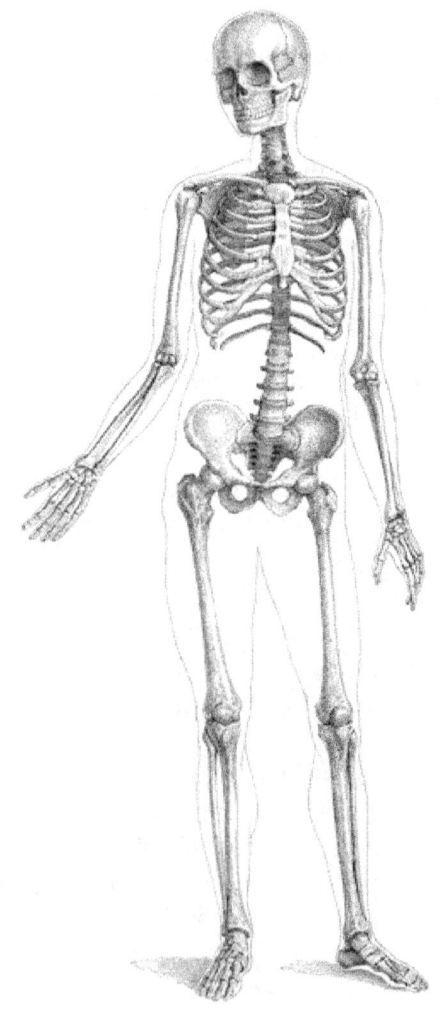

Monica A. Hand

DiVida hollows

she reverberates
she betweens
scoops out
sinks into
walls
she eyes hollow
she voice steams
she shadows her box

DiVida becomes pine

evergreen coniferous with needle-shaped leaves woody cones.
her thick and sticky sap turpentine her scent voluminous, audible

her arms her legs her buttocks her head her toes something to sit upon
soft like a cushion hard like the frame of a crypt

the wood of any pine is widely used
for shade for timber for tar inside its grove for languid longing

DiVida is all these things awkward and magnificent

get a grip Sapphire opines:
you is just like the rest of us beasts – you eat, you shit, and you pray

the Almighty won't smite you, accidentally, while he is tending his multitude
I got the secret for not getting lost in the fray – take the free

packets of needles 'n thread from motel bathrooms and the bars of soap too
let them who throw first stones at you be afraid

your plume's been bitchin' ever since the planet was covered in forest
and you really were a tree

a tree surrounded by water

Ramona McCallum

ASPIRATIONS

When breath exits
jaggedly,
like during sex
or through furious tears--

when it saws itself out
of your lungs as though air
itself is reluctant to leave,
then breath

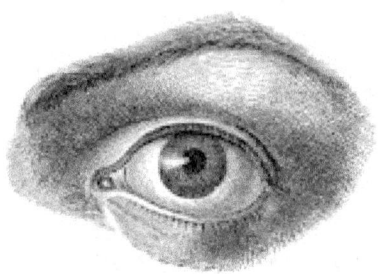

is like your soul

will be one day, a former occupant
pausing
for one last look at that room,
before it picks up its satchel,
turns around
and shuts the door.

Marguerite María Rivas

CASTING OFF THE SWADDLING OF IMMORTALITY

I want to rise up
from a cold stone-
padded river
swaddled in moss.

I want to push that bloody
vernix-covered swimmer—me
out of my own body.

I want to lick myself
clean of that cream
and the blood
and leave a pool of cool water
stillest in the ridge of
my infant fontanel.

To remind me to return
tadpole-like to that holy place
my soft skull cradled
by its lichenoid banks

Where each tufted patch of moss
is mine to eat
in green velvet purification.

Until my skull fuses
and rivulets stream cool
to open my eyes:

fontanel no more
true awareness gone
to die in the rational world.

Joanne G. Yoshida

SEVENTEEN
(from "Around the Fool Moon")

Can you teach me,
Ocean, how do you begin
Each wave
Where is the point that you
Lift up from your
Volumes
And rise one
Billowing sail
Fill it with
Breath and release it
Back into
Yourself

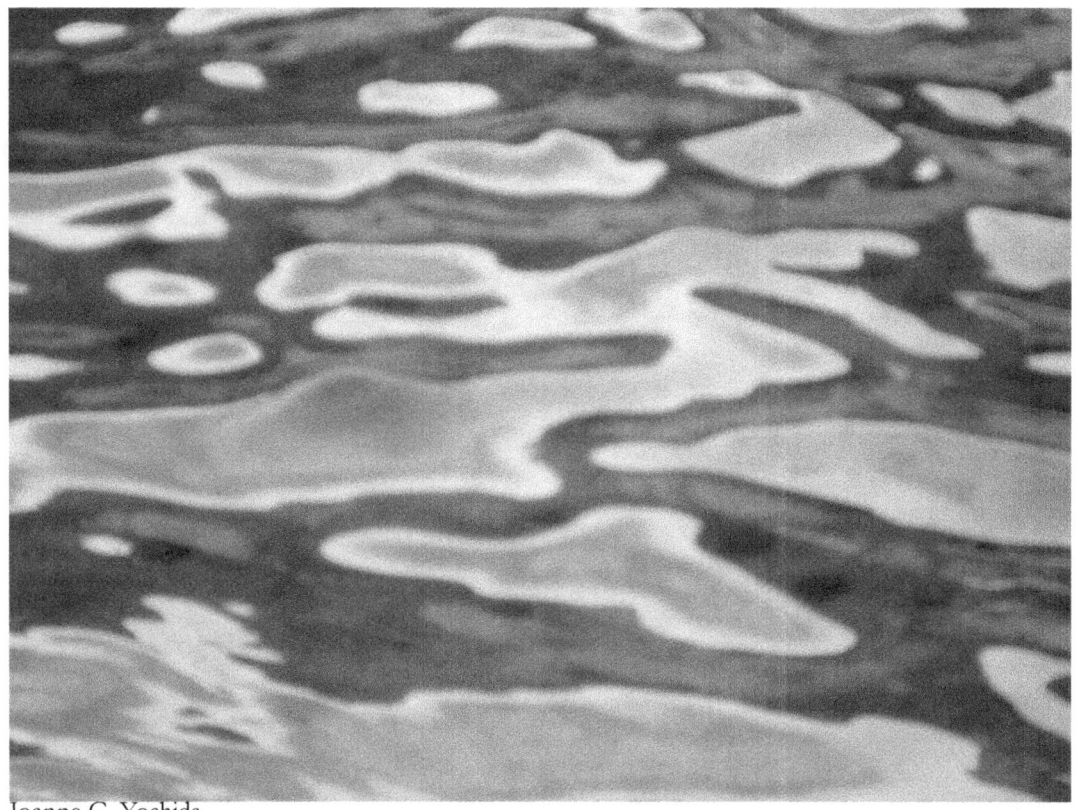

Joanne G. Yoshida

Adele Mendelson

VISITING EARTH

I borrowed a body for just a time
and visited Earth as an animal.
I lived in buildings, went to schools,
convened with others who, like me,
wore clothing and made plans.
Together we engaged
in all manner of distraction
to keep from the hole of wanting
at the center of things.

I coupled and bore children,
practiced housekeeping and economy,
all the while my wild blood
coursing, high fiery impulses
that could not be tamed.

I noted with anxiety the marking
of my time, not knowing how much
or how little I had to find
what would make me whole,
and take me home.

CONTRIBUTORS

Susan J. Allspaw currently lives in Colorado and works for the U.nited States Antarctic Program. Her poetry has appeared in *New England Review, Boulevard, Black Warrior Review, Borderlands: Texas Poetry Review, RATTLE,* and *Marlboro Review,* among others.

E.J. Antonio is a recipient of fellowships from the New York Foundation for the Arts, the Hurston/Wright Foundation and the Cave Canem Foundation. Her work has appeared online and has been published in various Journals and magazines. Her debut jazzoetry CD, *Rituals in the marrow: Recipe for a jam session* was released in the Fall of 2010. www.ejantoniobluez.net.

Felice Aull is retired faculty, New York University School of Medicine, where she is now adjunct, Division of Medical Humanities. She founded and is Editor Emerita of The Literature, Arts, and Medicine Database (http://litmed.med.nyu.edu/), a resource for medical humanities. A decade ago she began writing poetry and has poems in *Poet Lore, Margie, Ekphrasis, Umbrella,* and elsewhere. http://litmed.med.nyu.edu/ User?action=viewEditor&id=1.

Miriam Axel-Lute's favorite compliment is "I didn't think I liked poetry, but I liked that!" She has two daughters. Her poetry has been published here and there and performed from many stages, bookstore corners, classrooms, pulpits, and living rooms. She has three chapbooks, and her website is www.mjoy.org.

Linda Lee Ortiz Hughes Bakke lives and works in the San Francisco Bay Area. She is a photographer and a writer of fiction. http://lindabakke.com.

Kelly Bargabos lives and writes in Syracuse, New York and studies at the Downtown Writer's Center. Her work has appeared in newspapers and publications such as *The Mom Egg.* She enjoys writing about the things that move her and hopes they move you too.

Jessica Barksdale is the author of twelve novels (some under Jessica Inclan), including *Her Daughter's Eyes, The Matter of Grace,* and *When You Believe.* She is a professor of English at Diablo Valley College and teaches online novel writing for UCLA Extension. Visit her website: www.jessicabarksdaleinclan.com.

Virginia Bell's first book, *From the Belly,* is forthcoming from Sibling Rivalry Press in 2012. Her poetry has appeared in *CALYX , Poet Lore, Pebble Lake Review, Wicked Alice, Ekphrasis,* and other journals, and in the anthologies *Brute Neighbors* and *A Writers' Congress.* She is an editor with *RHINO* and an adjunct professor at Loyola University Chicago.

Eleanor Leonne Bennett is a 15 year old internationally award winning photographer and artist. Her photography has been published in the Telegraph , The Guardian, BBC News Website and on the cover of books and magazines in the United states and Canada. Her art has been exhibited in The Environmental Photographer of the year Exhibition (2011). www.eleanorleonnebennett.zenfolio.com.

Margo Berdeshevsky is the author of *Between Soul and Stone* and *But a Passage in Wilderness,* (Sheep Meadow Press) and *Beautiful Soon Enough.* Her honors include FC2's American Book Review/Ronald Sukenick/ Innovative Fiction Award for *Beautiful Soon Enough,* (University of Alabama Press/ 2009) and the Robert H. Winner Award from the Poetry Society of America, seven Pushcart Prize nominations, and two Pushcart "special mention" citations. Forthcoming: a cross-genre novel titled *Vagrant.* http://www.redroom.com/author/ margo-berdeshevsky.

Teresa Tumminello Brader, mother of two, was born in New Orleans and lives in the area still. Her stories and poems appear online and in print, most recently in *Halfway Down the Stairs* and in *Rejuvenation,* the 2011 journal of *All Rights Reserved.* http://teresa-nola.blogspot.com.

Melisa "Misha" Cahnmann-Taylor, is Professor of Language and Literacy Education at the University of Georgia. She is the winner of Dorothy Sargent Rosenberg Prizes and a Leeway Poetry Grant, and has co-authored two books: *Teachers Act Up: Creating Multicultural Learning Communities Through Theatre* and *Arts-Based Research in Education.* Her poems, articles, memoir and theatre games can be found at www.teachersactup.com.

Rosalie Calabrese is a native New Yorker and management consultant for the arts whose poetry has appeared in *Cosmopolitan, Poetry New Zealand, Poetica, Jewish Currents, Jewish Women's Literary Annual, And Then, Möbius, Genie, Thema, The Mom Egg, The New York Times, Critical Sociology, Psychoanalytic Perspectives* and several other publications, including anthologies and on the Web.

Valentina Cano is a student of classical singing who spends whatever free time she has either reading or writing. She lives in Miami, and you can find her here: http://carabosseslibrary.blogspot.com.

Janet Chalmers is a NY writer and photographer. She has written social and political commentary for many publications in the US and Mexico, as well as poems and reviews for *Barrow Street, Chelsea, Inkwell, The Mom Egg,* and *The Kenyon Review.* She is currently working on a chapbook, "In Remission", about her 106-year-old mother.

Sharon Charde, retired family therapist, women's writing workshop leader since 1990, award-winning poet with three published collections, one of which, *Branch In His Hand,* will be dramatized as a radio play for the BBC in 2012, has six Pushcart nominations and wide journal publication. www.SharonCharde.com.

Fay Chiang is a poet and visual artist who believes culture is a spiritual and psychological weapon used for the empowerment of people and communities. Working at Project Reach (www.projectreach.org), a youth center for young people at risk in Chinatown/Lower East Side, she is also a member of Zero Capital, a collective of artists (www.zerocapital.net); the Orchard Street Advocacy and Wellness Center, which supports people affected by HIV/AIDS, cancer and other chronic illnesses. Battling her 8th bout of breast cancer, she is completing China-town, a book-length poem and a memoir. *Seven Continents Nine Lives* was recently released by Bowery Books.

Laura A. Ciraolo was born in New York City and has lived and worked there as long as she can remember. She has three poems forthcoming in the *Avatar Review* this year. Most recently her poems have appeared in *The Centrifugal Eye, Orbis #155* (UK), *The Cortland Review #49, The New York Quarterly #66,* and *The Medulla Review.* She was a finalist for the 2010 Bordighera Poetry Prize.

Donna Coffey is an Associate Professor of English at Reinhardt University in North Georgia. She recently completed her MFA in Creative Writing at the Solstice Low Residency Program at Pine Manor College. Her poetry has appeared or is forthcoming in *Calyx, Prime Mincer, qarrtsiluni, The Honey Land Review* and *The Comstock Review.*

Nancy Cook currently lives in St. Paul. For years she has been attempting to integrate various parts of herself: sole parent, community lawyer, teacher, and writer. Her work has recently appeared or is forthcoming in a variety of literary and social policy journals, including the *Chrysalis Reader, Adventum, Nebo, Westward Quarterly, Emory Law Journal,* and *Prime Mincer.*

Hannah Craig lives in Pittsburgh, Pennsylvania. Her work has recently appeared in *Fence, Post Road,* the *American Literary Review,* the *Norton Anthology of Hint Fiction,* and elsewhere.

Anelie Crighton is an Australian Arts grad raising her little blonde bundle of energy in Germany who ekes out snippets of time to write between loads of laundry and rounds of raucous baby giggling. anelie.wordpress.com.

Barbara Crooker's poems have appeared in *The Green Mountains Review, The Denver Quarterly, Natural Bridge, The Beloit Poetry Journal, Poetry International, Poet Lore, The Valparaiso Poetry Review, South Carolina Review, Tar River Review, Nimrod, The Hollins Critic),* and the *Bedford Introduction to Literature,* and have been featured on *The Writer's Almanac* and *Verse Daily.* Her newest book is *More* (C&R Press, 2010). www.barbaracrooker.com.

Lesley Dame is a poet and full-time mama living in Michigan's Upper Peninsula. She is co-founder, poetry and nonfiction editor for *damselfly press,* and her poems have appeared in many online and print journals. http://www.wix.com/lesleydame/poet.

Kimberly Dark is a writer, mother, performer and professor. She is the author of five award-winning solo performance scripts and her poetry and prose appear in a number of publications. Kimberly's work engages audiences with surprising topics. Using humor and intimacy she reveals the contours of privilege and oppression in our daily lives. www.kimberlydark.com.

Holly Day is a housewife and mother of two living in Minneapolis, Minnesota. Her poetry has recently appeared in *Hawai'i Pacific Review, The Oxford American,* and *Slipstream.* Her book publications include *Music Composition for Dummies, Guitar-All-in-One for Dummies,* and *Music Theory for Dummies,* which has recently been translated into French, Dutch, Spanish, Russian, and Portuguese.

A five-time Pushcart nominee, Liz Dolan has won a $6,000 established artist fellowship from the Delaware Division of the Arts, 2009. Her second poetry manuscript, *A Secret of Long Life,* which is seeking a publisher, was nominated for the Robert McGovern Prize. Her first poetry collection, *They Abide,* was recently published by March Street Press.

Rachel Dorroh's writing is often inspired by her two children, husband, and vegetable garden. The poem in this issue is dedicated to the community of mothers she is a part of in small-town Kentucky. Her recent poetry and prose has appeared in *Hip Mama* and *Hobby Farm Home,* respectively.

Jessica Dyer received an MFA from Columbia College Chicago where she happens to work a day job. Her poetry has appeared in *Columbia Poetry Review, Arsenic Lobster, PANK, So to Speak, North American Review,* and a Star Trek-themed magazine called *Make it So.*

Kathy Engel is a poet, teacher, activist, and of course, a mom. She is co founder, with Alexis De Veaux, of Lyrical Democracies (www.lyricaldemocracies.com), teaches in NYU's Art and Public Policy Program, and is on the Board of The Young People's Project.

Kate Falvey's work has appeared in a number of print and online journals, including *Memoir(and), Danse Macabre, Subliminal Interiors, Hoboeye, Umbrella, CRIT, Inscribed, Hearing Voices, OVS, Literary Mama, Women Writers, and Fringe.* She is on the editorial board of the N.Y.U. Langone Medical Center's *Bellevue Literary Review* and is Editor-in-Chief of the *2 Bridges Review.* She teaches at City Tech/CUNY and lives with her daughter in Long Beach, New York. http://www.2bridgesreview.org.

Jessica Feder-Birnbaum is a writer, teacher, and theater arts specialist. Her passion is to build community through words and theater. Her plays, stories, and video scripts have been commissioned by resident theater and dance companies, universities, comedy troupes, and childrens book publishers; her articles on family and parenting topics have appeared in print and on-line media. Jessica is a New York State Council of the Arts MFTA summer institute scholarship recipient.

Stephanie Feuer's articles and essays have appeared in *The New York Times, The New York Daily News, The Boston Herald, Sojourner, Bettyconfidential.com,* and numerous anthologies. She's read her work at KGB, The Bowery Poetry Club, in the "See Me, Hear Me" show, and in several venues with the talented writers of *The Mom Egg.* Stephanie recently completed a YA novel.

Kathleen Flenniken's poems have appeared most recently in *Poetry Northwest, Alaska Quarterly Review, Tar River Poetry,* and the 2012 Pushcart Prize Anthology. Her second book, *Plume,* a personal history of the Hanford Nuclear Site, is newly released from University of Washington Press. Please visit www.kathleenflenniken.com.

Sandra Florence received her Masters in Creative Writing/Poetry from San Francisco State University. She has been teaching and writing for over 30 years. She taught at the University of Arizona in Tucson for eighteen years, and a number of venues throughout the community working with refugees, the homeless, adolescent-parents, women in recovery and youth at risk. She currently teaches writing and literature at Pima Community College.

Linda McCauley Freeman has an MFA in Writing from Bennington College. The poet-in-residence for the Putnam County Arts Council for five years, she is a columnist for *Living & Being* magazine and three-time winner of the Talespinners Short Story contest. She has been published in many literary journals and anthologized in GIRLS: An Anthology. She is working on a novel.

Eleanor Gaffney is a teacher and poet. She has a MAW from Manhattanville College and her poems have been published in *Alimentum, The Westchester Review*, and *The Mom Egg*. She teaches English to recent immigrants, both adults and teens. She and her husband Bill live in Nyack, NY and have two adult sons.

Ana Garza G'z is a translator and community interpreter living and working in central California. Her work has appeared in various journals and anthologies, most recently in *Occupy Poetry, Magnolia Journal*, and *Taktil*.

Nancy Gerber continues to write about motherhood though her kids are 26 and 21. Once a mother, always a mother, says her 90-year-old mother-in-law, Evelyn Gerber, and she should know.

Therese Gilardi is a poet, essayist and novelist (*Matching Wits With Venus*) whose work has appeared in *Literary Mama, Punchnel's, The Dirty Napkin, Knowing Pains, So Far and Yet So Near: Stories of Americans Abroad*, and other print and electronic publications. Therese lives with her husband, children, dogs, tortoise and hare in the hills above Los Angeles.

Heather Haldeman lives in Pasadena, California and began writing professionally eleven years ago. She has been married to her husband, Hank, for thirty-three years and has three grown children. Her work has been published in *The Christian Science Monitor, Chicken Soup for the Soul, From Freckles to Wrinkles, Grandmother Earth, The Mom Egg* and numerous online journals. She has received first, second and third prizes for her essays.

Monica A Hand is a poet and book artist who is exploring a nomadic lifestyle. Her manuscript, *me and Nina* received a 2010 Kinereth Gensler Award from Alice James Books, available January 2012. Her poems have appeared in numerous publications including *Naugatuck River Review, The Sow's Ear, Drunken Boat*, and *Gathering Ground: A Reader Celebrating Cave Canem's First Decade*. She holds a MFA in Poetry and Poetry in Translation from Drew University.

Lois Marie Harrod's *The Only Is* won the 2012 Tennessee Chapbook Contest (Poems & Plays), her eleventh book *Brief Term*, a collection of poems about teachers and teaching was published by Black Buzzard Press, 2011, and her *Cosmongony* won the 2010 Hazel Lipa Chapbook (Iowa State). She teaches Creative Writing at The College of New Jersey. www.loismarieharrod.com.

JP Howard aka Juliet P. Howard is a mom of two awesome sons, a poet, lawyer and Cave Canem fellow. She is a Lambda Literary Foundation 2011 Emerging LGBT Voices Fellow. She co-founded Women Writers in Bloom Poetry Salon & Blog, a forum offering women writers at all levels a venue to come together in a positive and supportive space. http://womenwritersinbloompoetrysalon.blogspot.com/.

TT Jax is a parent, partner, mixed-media artist, and Pushcart-nominated writer currently living in the Pacific Northwest by way of 28 years in the deep South.

Danielle Jones-Pruett is an MFA candidate at UMass Boston, where she also teaches creative writing. Her work has recently appeared, or is forthcoming, in *Cider Press Review, First Inkling, Southern Women's Review*, and others.

Heidi Joseph is a poet, artist, elementary school educator and mother to three children. She lives with her family, two dogs and six chickens in Novato, California. Her work has appeared in *The Marin Poetry Center Anthology, Poetry Farmer's Almanac, Plasma* and *The Northridge Review*.

Kelli Stevens Kane's poetry manuscript, *Hallelujah Science*, was selected as a Finalist for the 2011 Four Way Books Levis Poetry Prize, and a Semifinalist for the Persea Books 2011 Lexi Rudnitsky First Book Prize in Poetry. In 2011 she received an Advancing Black Arts in Pittsburgh grant, and fellowships from the August Wilson Center, Cave Canem, and Flight School. www.kellistevenskane.com.

Donna Katzin is Executive Director of Shared Interest, a non-profit investment fund that advances equitable development in Southern Africa's communities of color. Her poetry is informed by her work, her family and struggles for social justice. Recently she published *With These Hands*, a collection of poems about South Africa's deeply human and poetic process of giving birth to itself. For more information visit www.sharedinterest.org.

Molly Sutton Kiefer's chapbook *The Recent History of Middle Sand Lake* won the 2010 Astounding Beauty Ruffian Press Poetry Award. Her work has appeared in *Harpur Palate, Gulf Stream, Wicked Alice, Breakwater Review,* and *Permafrost,* among others. She currently lives in Minnesota with her husband and daughter, where she is at work on a manuscript on (in)fertility. In addition, she serves as assistant poetry editor to *Midway Journal,* and curates *Balancing the Tide: Motherhood and the Arts | An Interview Project.* More can be found at mollysuttonkiefer.com.

Martha Kinkade is an author, a healer, an educator dedicated to promoting a peaceful and harmonious way of living. Her first book of poems, *Winter's Light,* she writes about growing up in Wyoming. Her poetry has appeared in *Psychic Meatloaf, Jackson Hole Review* and *San Diego Writer's Ink Anthology.* She lives, writes and teaches at San Diego State University. www.marthakinkade.com.

Evelyn Krampf is a California native who writes, lives and teaches in Berlin. After graduating from U.C. Berkeley, she worked in the non-profit sector for a few years before deciding to move to Europe to pursue her writing.

Jack Kristiansen exists in the notebooks and computer files of William Aarnes. Kristiansen's poems have appeared in the *Tipton Poetry Journal, Sunsets and Silencers, Fogged Clarity,* and *FIELD.*

Carol Levin's chapbooks: *Red Rooms and Others* (Pecan Grove Press, 2009) and *Sea Lions Sing Scat* (Finishing Line Press). Forthcoming is full volume: *Stunned By the Velocity* (Pecan Grove). She's been published in literary journals and anthologies. She's an Editorial Assistant at Crab Creek Review and teaches The Breathing Lab / Alexander Technique, in Seattle www.the-breathing-lab.com.

Amanda Regan Lighthiser earned her MFA in fiction at the University of Oregon. Her work has appeared in *The Inkwater Ink Anthology* and *Voix du Vieux.* She lives in New Orleans, where she teaches writing and is at work on her second novel.

Tsaurah Litzky writes erotica, fiction, creative nonfiction,book reviews and art crticism and the occasional play. Poetry, however, is her heart and she has published fifteen poetry chapbooks and two major poetrycollections. The first was *Baby On The Water* put out by Long Shot Press. Bowery Books has just published Tsaurah's new collection, *Cleaning The Duck.*

Ellaraine Lockie has recently received the Best Individual Collection Award from *Purple Patch* and won the San Gabriel Poetry Festival Chapbook Contest. Her latest chapbook,*Wild as in Familiar,* has just been released by Finishing Line Press. Ellaraine teaches poetry workshops and serves as Poetry Editor for the lifestyles magazine, *Lilipoh.*

Katie Manning lives in Louisiana with her husband and son. She is Editor-in-Chief of *Rougarou* and a doctoral fellow in English at UL-Lafayette. Her writing has been published in *New Letters, PANK, The Pedestal Magazine, Poet Lore,* and *So to Speak,* among other journals and anthologies, and she is the 2011 winner of *The Nassau Review's* Author Award for Poetry.

Lucia May is a violinist and poet who lives in St. Paul, MN. Her poems have appeared or are forthcoming in *Main Channel Voices, Pemmican, Evening Street Review, Hot Metal Press, Burnt Bridge, Paperdarts, Talking Stick, Tall Grass, the Prose-Poem Project,* and *Little Red Tree International Poetry Prize Anthology: 2010, The Widows' Handbook, The Awakenings Review.*

Ramona McCallum, along with spouse, ceramic sculptor Brian K. McCallum, raise their six children and make art in Garden City, Kansas. Ramona's poetry collection, *Still Life with Dirty Dishes* is forthcoming from Woodley Press. For fun, Ramona's establishing a covert creative writing curriculum within the public school system. Check out her poetic endeavors, disguised as a substitute teacher, at thesubversecity.com.

Leslie Anne Mcilroy won the 1997 Slipstream Poetry Chapbook Prize for *Gravel,* the 2001 Word Press Poetry Prize for her full-length collection *Rare Space* and the 1997 Chicago Literary Awards. Her second book, *Liquid Like This,* was published by Word Press in 2008. Leslie works as a copywriter in Pittsburgh, PA. Learn more about Leslie's poems and performances at lamcilroy.com.

Adele Mendelson was born in Ohio and now lives in Oakland, California. She taught English at the University of California at Berkeley for many years and now gives her time to writing both fiction and poetry and helping other people do the same. She has produced several volumes of poetry and reads her work at venues around the Bay Area.

A native of Lowell, Massachusetts, Matt Miller is a former Wallace Stegner Fellow in Poetry at Stanford University. He is the author of Cameo Diner: Poems. His second book, *Club Icarus*, won the 2012 Vassar Miller Poetry Prize and will be published next year by University of North Texas Press. He lives, works, and surfs in New Hampshire with his wife Emily and their two children.

Leah Mooney writes poems and fiction in the small-town wilds of western Wisconsin, where she lives with her family and holds down a day job. Her work has most recently appeared or is forthcoming at *Literary Mama, Tilt-a-Whirl, Atticus Review, Fiction365* and *BOXCAR Poetry Review.* anvilsandedelweiss.blogspot.com.

Jacqui Morton lives in Massachusetts with her husband and their toddler. She holds an MFA in Creative Writing from Antioch University, Los Angeles and a day job, and writes every moment she can. Her poems have also been published or are forthcoming in *Recovering the Self: A Journal of Hope and Healing,* and *The Provo Orem Word.*

Ariana Nadia Nash is the winner of the 2011 Philip Levine Poetry Prize and her first book of poetry is forthcoming from Anhinga Press. Ariana completed her MFA in creating writing at the University of North Carolina Wilmington, and spent the fall of 2011 in residence at The MacDowell Colony. Her poetry has recently been published in *The Café Review, Rock & Sling, Main Street Rag,* and *2River View.*

Sandra Ramos O'Briant's work has appeared in *Café Irreal, Flashquake, riverbabble, In Posse, LiteraryMama, Whistling Shade, La Herencia, latinola.com,* and *The Copperfield Review.* In addition, her short stories have been anthologized in *Best Lesbian Love Stories of 2004, What Wildness is This: Women Write About the Southwest* (University of Texas Press, Spring 2007), *Latinos in Lotus Land: An Anthology of Contemporary Southern California Literature,* (Bilingual Press, 2008), *Hit List: The Best of Latino Mystery* (Arte Publico (2009), and *The Mom Egg* (Half Shell Press, 2010). Read her work at www.thesandovalsisters.com and www.bloodmother.com.

Eve Packer, Bronx-born, poet/performer--three books, *skulls head samba, playland poems 1994-2004,* and the most recent, *new nails* (all Fly By Night Press). She has 4 poetry/jazz CD's with the saxophonist Noah Howard; spring will see a new poetry/jazz CD with pianist Stephanie Stone and multi-instrumentalist Daniel Carter. Eve has one son, one grandson (so far), lives downtown and swims daily.

Carl Palmer, twice nominated for the Micro Award and thrice for the Pushcart Prize by poetry magazine editors, is from Old Mill Road in Ridgeway, VA. Carl now lives in University Place, WA. MOTTO: *Long Weekends Forever* http://brightlightmultimedia.com/BLCafe/ShowcasedTalent-CarlPalmerPoemsStories.htm#Poems.

Angela S. Patane teaches English, fronts a band called The Young Dead, and publishes a zine called *Love Your Rebellion.* If she's not hard at work pursuing her dreams, she is spending time with her two cats and her loving partner.

Theta Pavis is a poet, blogger and award-winning journalist. A graduate of UCLA and the Columbia School of Journalism, she lives in Jersey City with her husband, 7-year-old daughter, and a cat named Luna. Her poems have appeared in numerous journals, including the *Journal of New Jersey Poets* and are forthcoming in *Pulse.*

Puma Perl is a performance artist and a widely published poet and writer. She is the author of the award-winning chapbook *Belinda and Her Friends* and the full-length collection *knuckle tattoos,* and has a new chapbook, *Ruby True,* coming out shortly. She is the co-creator, co-producer, and main curator of DDAY Productions, which currently puts on shows at 3 venues, including a monthly all-female production at the Bowery Poetry Club.

Kyle Potvin's poetry has appeared in *Measure, Tygerburning Literary Journal, The Mom Egg, JAMA, Literary Mama, Blue Unicorn* and *The New York Times'* "Well" blog. She was a finalist for the 2008 Howard Nemerov Sonnet Award. Her chapbook, "Sound Travels on Water," is scheduled for publication by Finishing Line Press in 2012.

Jessy Randall is married with two children, lives in Colorado, and works as a rare books librarian. Her collection of poems *Injecting Dreams into Cows* is forthcoming from Red Hen Press in fall 2012. Her website is http://personalwebs.coloradocollege.edu/~jrandall/.

Diane Raptosh has published three books of poems: Just West of Now (Guernica Editions, 1992), Labor Songs (Guernica, 1999), and Parents from a Different Alphabet (Guernica, 2008). Her fourth book, American Amnesiac, is coming out in 2013 with Etruscan Press. The recipient of three Literature Fellowships from the Idaho Commission on the Arts, she teaches creative writing and literature at The College of Idaho. She lives in Boise with her family.

Christine Redman-Waldeyer, Founder of *Adanna,* a women's literary journal, is an Assistant Professor at Passaic County Community College. She earned her doctorate in Writing from Drew University. Her publications include *Frame by Frame, Gravel,* and *Eve Asks* with Muse Pie Press. She was a featured poet for the Poetry Project founded by Dr. Mary Ann Miller at Caldwell College in 2011. http://adannajournal.blogspot.com.

Marguerite María Rivas teaches in NYC. A recipient of numerous grants and awards, her poetry has been published in *Earth's Daughters, Acentos Review, Short, Fast, and Deadly*, and *Más Tequila Review*. A book of poems, *Tell No One: Poems of Witness* (Chimbarazu Press) will be published in spring 2012.

John Rodriguez holds a Ph.D. in English from The CUNY Graduate Center.
His poetry has recently appeared in the anthology *One Word: Contemporary Writers on the Words They Love or Loathe* and the journals *PALABRA* and *Obscura*. He teaches at Queensborough Community College as an assistant professor, and lives in The Bronx, New York.

Helen Ruggieri has a new book - *Butterflies Under a Japanese Moon* - from Kitsune Books or visit www.HelenRuggieri.com.

Susan Rukeyser earned her MA in Creative Writing from Lancaster University, UK. Her work appears in *Atticus Review, Eclectic Flash, Ink Sweat and Tears, Melusine, Metazen, PANK, Short Fast and Deadly*, and *SmokeLong Quarterly*. She won *Hippocampus Magazine*'s 2011 "Remember in November" Contest for Creative Non-Fiction. She does her best to explain herself here: www.susanrukeyser.com.

Nina Schuyler's novel, *The Painting*, was nominated for the Northern California Book Award and has been translated into four languages. Her next novel, *Accidental Birds*, will be out spring, 2012. Her short stories have been nominated for a Pushcart Prize. She teaches creative writing at the University of San Francisco. www.ninaschuyler.com.

Lani Scozzari holds a BFA from Emerson College as well as the MFA from Sarah Lawrence, where she served at the editor of *Lumina*, their literary magazine. *Ballet's Children* was awarded a Massachusetts Cultural Council Finalist Grant. Publications include *Comstock Review, DeComp, Whistling Fire, Saw Palm,*and several anthologies. She is mother to two daughters, ages 3 and 2. You can read more at Teandteadventures.blogspot.com.

Leah Sewell is a Chicago native living in Topeka, Kansas. She is the founding editor of *XYZ Magazine*, a freelance graphic designer and the founder and mediator of the Topeka Writers' Workshop. Her poems have appeared in journals including *Flint Hills Review, Blue Island Review, Midwestern Gothic* and *Begin Again: 150 Kansas Poems*.

Debora Bess Siegel holds a BFA from The Cooper Union, MLA from Empire State College and a teaching certificate from David Yellin College. She is a teacher trainer at the Hebrew University and teaches at the Hebrew University Secondary School. An active member of the Jerusalem Writers Group, she has had short stories published in *First Writer Magazine* and the *Ranfurly Review*.

Judith Skillman has authored twelve collections of poetry, including *The Never* (Dream Horse Press, 2010) and *The White Cypress* (Cervéna Barva Press, 2011). Her poetry and translations have appeared in *Poetry, FIELD, The Iowa Review, Prairie Schooner, The Midwest Quarterly, The Southern Review,* and elsewhere. A former editor of *Fine Madness,* Skillman has taught at City University and Richard Hugo House. www.judithskillman.com.

Golda Solomon, poet, performer, professor, hosts Po'Jazz, formerly at Cornelia Street Café, now traveling to various venues. Her latest collection: *Medicine Woman of Jazz* (World Audience Publishers) available early 2012. Golda is a poetry outreach mentor for City College and Poet-In-Residence at Blue Door Gallery, Yonkers, New York where she facilitates ArtSpeak:Responding to the Walls, ekphrastic workshops. www.jazzjaunts.com; www.bluedoorgallery.org.

Cassie Premo Steele has published eight books in several genres, writes a monthly column at www.LiteraryMama.com called "Birthing the Mother Writer," and works as a writing & creativity coach, locally and long-distance, from her Co-Creating Studio in South Carolina. Her next book, a poetry collection about mothering called *The Pomegranate Papers*, will be published in April. Her website is www.cassiepremosteele.com.

Christine Stewart-Nuñez is the author of *Snow, Salt, Honey* (Red Dragonfly Press 2012), *Keeping Them Alive* (WordTech Editions 2011), *Postcard on Parchment* (ABZ Press 2008), *Unbound & Branded* (Finishing Line Press 2006), and *The Love of Unreal Things* (Finishing Line Press 2005). She teaches in the English Department at South Dakota State University.

Patricia Thomas was born and raised in southern Alabama. She earned a B.A. and Master's degree from Auburn University and a Ph.D. from Texas A&M University. She has taught at Loyola Marymount University, the University of Southern California, and Texas A&M. Her essays and stories have been published in *Deep South Magazine, Muscadine Lines: A Southern Journal,* and *Front Porch Review,* to name a few. She currently teaches writing at Fullerton College in California. http://www.patriciathomaswritings.com.

Claudia Van Gerven teaches writing in Boulder, Colorado. Her poems have been published in a number of journals including *Prairie Schooner* and *Calyx.* Her work has appeared in numerous anthologies and has been nominated for the Push Cart Prize. Her chapbook, *The Ends of Sunbonnet Sue,* won the Angel Fish Press Poetry Prize. Her most recent chapbook is, *Amazing Grace,* (Green Fuse Poetic Arts, 2010).

Cynthia Veach's poetry has appeared in many journals including *Chelsea, Prairie Schooner, Chicago Review, Carolina Quarterly, Poet Lore, Sow's Ear Poetry Review, WomenArts Quarterly Review,* and *Weave Magazine.* She lives in Manchester, Massachusetts. http://52poemsproject.blogspot.com.

Nancy Vona's work has been published in *Rushlight, Literary Mama,* and *The Mom Egg.* She finds time to write whenever she can climb out of the sinkhole of elementary school volunteer activities. She lives with her husband, two sons, and dog in Massachusetts. She is grateful to *The Mom Egg* for supporting and celebrating the voices of mother artists and writers.

Toni L. Wilkes' chapbook *Black Water Beneath a Lid of Ice* (Finishing Lines Press) received honorable mention in the 2010 New Women's Voices. *Stepping Through Moons* (Finishing Line Press) was nominated for the California Book Award and the PEN USA Literary Award. A Pushcart Prize and Best of the Net nominee, Wilkes is the editor of *In Posse Review.* http://tonilwilkes.wordpress.com.

Dallas Woodburn is the author of two collections of short stories and editor of *Dancing With The Pen: a collection of today's best youth writing.* A Pushcart Prize nominee, she is also the recipient of the Ninth Glass Woman Prize and the Brian Mexicott Playwriting Award. She teaches creative writing and composition at Purdue University. Website: www.dallaswoodburn.com.

Joanne G. Yoshida lives in Oita, Japan with her husband and daughter. She recently began to teach Shake Your Soul/Kripalu Yoga Dance, through which she is enjoying deepening her connection to her body, her spirit and the world around her. http://aikawarazulifeinjapan.blogspot.com.

Maya Jewell Zeller's first book, *Rust Fish,* was released in 2011 from Lost Horse Press. Individual poems have won awards from several magazines, most recently *Sycamore Review,* and appear widely. Maya lives in Spokane with her husband and daughter, and teaches English at Gonzaga University. More about Maya can be found at http://mayajewellzeller.wordpress.com.

www.ingramcontent.com/pod-product-compliance
Lightning Source LLC
Chambersburg PA
CBHW081324020726
47506CB00005B/1174